Country Towns
of
MICHIGAN

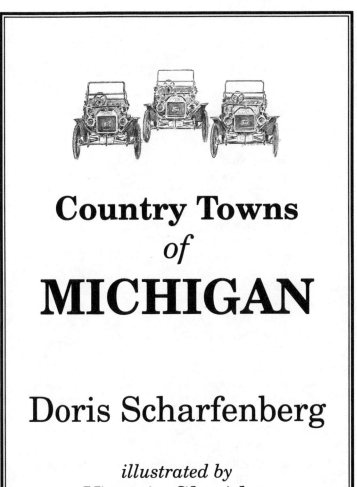

Country Towns
of
MICHIGAN

Doris Scharfenberg

illustrated by
Victoria Sheridan

Country Roads Press
CASTINE, MAINE

Country Towns of Michigan

Published by Country Roads Press
P.O. Box 286, Lower Main Street
Castine, Maine 04421

Text and cover design by Janet Patterson
Illustrations by Victoria Sheridan
Typesetting by Typeworks

ISBN 1-56626-048-5

Library of Congress Cataloging-in-Publication Data

Scharfenberg, Doris, 1925–
    Country towns of Michigan / Doris Scharfenberg ; illustrator,
Victoria Sheridan.
        p.   cm.
    Includes index.
    ISBN 1-56626-048-5 : $9.95
    1. Michigan—Guidebooks.   2. Cities and towns—Michigan—
Guidebooks.   I. Title.
F564.3.S27   1994b
917.4704 ′43—dc20   93-49834
                                                                    CIP

Printed in the United States of America.
10   9   8   7   6   5   4   3   2   1

To Muriel

Contents

Introduction

In this random sampling of Michigan communities there is much variety and much that is the same. I looked for towns with populations of 7,000 or under, interesting histories, geographical features, festivals that far out-scaled the community's size, etc. I didn't have to look far; Michigan is blessed with hundreds of towns with charm and surprising vigor.

Some of these towns are on one of the Great Lakes; that's the kind of "country" Michigan lives with.

I rather deplore the way fast-food restaurants, discount stores, and chain names have made all towns too much alike. Once past the boom-box mentality and identical strip-mall façades, however, I found a lot of individuality; reassuring numbers of preservation-minded, land-loving, family-oriented nice folks.

It was fun, but disturbing that I couldn't do them all. Apologies to Adrian, Hillsdale, Allegan, Armada, Lapeer, St. Johns, Roscommon, Grayling, Newaygo, St. Ignace, Mackinaw City, Gladwin, Mainstique, Bessemer . . .

That, however, is how second books get started.

Many thanks to the chambers of commerce, to the Michigan Travel Bureau, to friends in eighty-three counties.

D.S.

1

Bad Axe: Michigan Thumb Print

No, Bad Axe is not a translation of an Indian word meaning "busted tomahawk." It came from an English message on a piece of paper, maybe joked about by those who read the notation. Like a wire tied around a sapling; if no one moves the wire the tree will enclose the strange ring and adapt.

That's how it was with Bad Axe. On an early map of the east-west trail across Michigan's "Thumb," where it crossed a north-south path, surveyor Rudolf Papst found an axe with a broken handle in an abandoned hunter's camp. It was duly noted on his map . . . and stayed there for other maps yet to come.

In the 1950s entertainer Arthur Godfrey wrote a silly song called "I Met My Baby In Bad Axe" which gave the town its fifteen minutes of fame. The song is forgotten, but the name has become one that Michiganians are rather proud of.

As a busy shopping center, the seat of Huron County, and the hub of a very special farm and recreation area, Bad Axe presides over life at the tip of the Thumb, the peninsula giving lower Michigan the shape of a mitten. Without interstate traffic or heavy population, the region is as remote from big-biz bustle as if it were on the moon, yet close to southeast Michigan's metro areas. It's a big-lake getaway place only a few hundred miles from Detroit's City Hall.

About 3,300 people call Bad Axe home. Simple, unpretentious, homey, plain, and neat. Tree-lined streets put on a great color show during the fall. But the special secret of Bad Axe appeal is one-on-one friendliness and citizens who include the world in their family. On the Welcome-to-Bad-Axe sign at city limits are logos of the Lions Club, Jaycees, chamber of commerce (two C's on an axe with a broken handle), and Rotary International (there are more).

The sign also holds up a picture of a useless axe bending unnaturally out of a tree stump, apt reminders of times gone by. Like the rest of Michigan, the Thumb wore a thick cover of forest in the early 1800s. Lumbering took charge of commerce, and settlements along Lake Huron (Port Sanilac, Port Hope, Port Austin) shipped wood to a waiting world.

Then disaster almost eliminated the timber trade overnight when too little rain in the summer of 1871 dried up wells and creeks, and the woods crackled with brittleness. Piles of sawdust around lumber mills became explosive—and hazardous. Over in Illinois and Wisconsin things were even worse. Whether it was Mrs. O'Leary's cow kicking over the lantern that started the great 1871 Chicago fire or not, this part of the Midwest was set for tragedy, just waiting for a careless act or stray bolt of lightning. As Chicago burned, horrendous fires in northern Wisconsin killed hundreds. Sparked by super-heated air or burning airborne debris (theories vary), Holland and several other Michigan cities on Lake Michigan were nearly destroyed by flames that went leapfrogging across the state.

A second fire in 1873 finished lumbering as a major industry. Farming and commercial fishing took up the slack.

Forty years later, another calamity. One of the worst November gales in Great Lakes history sank eight ships with all hands, wrecked a dozen others, and wiped out all fishing ports on lower Lake Huron; there wasn't even one dock for the increasing number of lake pleasure-steamers.

Away from shore, the storm had a ripple effect in slowing the growth of towns like Bad Axe, while boosting the importance of agriculture.

The Axe is essentially a farm town with additional assignments: tourism and county government. Farms spread for miles around the wide and fertile terrain, dotted with some areas of woods and small lakes. There are 175 Centennial Farms in Huron County, twenty-five of them dating back to the 1850s and 85 percent still owned by their original families. That's a settling-in way above average. Besides fruit, pumpkins, peas, and corn, sugar beets and white navy beans are big cash crops.

Roads into Bad Axe run as straight as yardsticks across a tabletop, dull only to the unseeing. There is a pleasing geometry in a terrain without frills, with bonus moments when red barns of cathedral size catch the low beams of a setting sun and seem to glow on their own.

From Detroit, State 53 (Van Dyke Road) becomes West Huron inside the Bad Axe boundaries, and makes a left turn in the middle of town to continue north. It takes effort to get lost.

On a walk around the shopping blocks, posters either urge you to join "Cruise Night" ("two days of summer fun and excitement for the antique car enthusiast") or they announce the county fair. Huron County's one and only movie house, the Bad Axe Theater on East Huron, has been divided into two showcases for first-run flicks. The former balcony, now a theater on its own, is *tiny*, but you get used to that.

Shops understandably lean heavily toward sporting goods. About twenty miles north, the Thumb rounds out at Port Austin where there is a great fishing pier. It is just about the same distance to Harbor Beach on Lake Huron as to the shores of Saginaw Bay. Fishing docks, deer hunting, and the marshlands beloved by duck hunters abound. Huron County's crescent shore is ninety-three miles long, full of public beaches in eight county and two state parks, and it has twelve boat launching sites.

Five rough-hewn log buildings across from the public library on South Hanselman Street are early area structures, restored and brought here to form the Pioneer Log Cabin Village Museum. A blacksmith shop, chapel, general store, barn, one-room schoolhouse, and cabin home stand in a small circle as if they were ready for business. Bowls, blankets, slates, forge, or whatever, the rooms have been furnished with things needed to keep body and

One of many working farms

soul together. If you want to rent the chapel for your own wedding, just ask.

Museum hours are a slight problem, open only on Sundays during summer weekends—not much of a time slot for stopping by. With luck the hours will have expanded by the time this guide goes to press.

Their high school teams may run up a disdainful competition, but all of the towns in Huron County are linked so closely to Bad Axe they are like other rooms in the same house. Pigeon, about twenty miles west on State 142, has twice as many logos on its welcome sign but half the population. They are mighty proud of their grain elevator, the largest in Michigan; its contents may contribute heavily to your next can of bean or barley soup. For more regional history visit the Pigeon Historical Depot Museum.

Sebewaing, a jog southwest on Saginaw Bay, is an Indian word for "crooked river." A big sugar mill looms over the town where a sweet annual Michigan Sugar Festival in late June celebrates the product. Mentioning sugar substitutes is considered rotten manners, but talk fishing all you want. The bay has been a favorite walleye and bass convention center luring anglers for generations. Just north in Caseville, a small amount of commercial fishing still goes on; here you can hunker into the Bay Port Fish Company for fresh-caught dinner fixings.

On the "Grade A" pleasant State 25 route around the Thumb, Caseville has a natural edge: two state parks with wide beaches and low dunes, plus the Huron County Wilderness Arboretum and Nature Center which is nine miles from town on Loosemore Road. The center comprises 180 acres and self-guided trails for nature lovers and environmentalists to enjoy.

(There are more motels and places to stay on this side of the Thumb than on the Lake Huron side; consider this if you are planning a two-day jaunt.)

The sun rises and sets on Port Austin, Thumb tip town, where a *long* pier stretches far out to meet both bay and lake. There are two great places for dinner. One is The Bank 1884, seating by reservation only—when they are open. (Well, you know how

5

banker's hours are!) The two-story brick building, handsomely restored by two Huron County residents, seats you on old church pews near brass teller's cages, etc. Oysters, trout, etc., are superbly done. Put money in The Bank, located on Lake Street (State 53 or the road to Bad Axe). Telephone 517-738-5353.

The other spot, the spectacular Garfield Inn, radiates French Victorian charm. Years ago President James A. Garfield visited frequently; once he delivered a speech endorsing Gen. Ulysses S. Grant for president from its third-floor balcony. Today a bed and breakfast *experience*, the Garfield serves gourmet dinners to non-guests as well. Highlights on the menu range from lobster chowder to New Zealand venison; excellent. Along with The Bank, the Garfield is also located on Lake Street. Reservations are highly recommended. Telephone 517-738-5254.

Continuing around, visit Grind Stone City; no city to be found but some of the grindstones once made here are still lying around. Also visit the Huron City Museum, where again there is no city but more country buildings (most on their original sites) full of area history. A U.S. Coast Guard Rescue Station and the "House of Seven Gables" (name inspired by the house in Salem, Massachusetts) are among the highlights here. Open July 1 to Labor Day. Admission is charged; telephone 517-428-4123.

A little farther down the coast, spot a photogenic lighthouse (aren't they all?) now part of a summer-only marine museum. Stop at the park just before you reach Port Hope.

Harbor Beach, a pretty place with a lot of marina facilities, is the largest town on the Lake Huron side of the Thumb and home of former governor and U. S. Supreme Court Justice Frank Murphy. Be sure to see the murals on the side of the Community House, then go in and find out about the sports and craft events around town.

From Harbor Beach it is eighteen miles back to Bad Axe, ending a full-circle trip that can be done in an afternoon . . . unless you stop at one of the six Huron County golf courses.

Bad Axe: Michigan Thumb Print

If high excitement is what you're after, try another town. Bad Axe, however, is the essence of Thumb life, a slower lane.

Tourism Hot Line: 1-800-35-THUMB
Bad Axe Chamber of Commerce: 517-269-9918

2

Calumet and
Laurium: Sister Act

Was life *that* much simpler in the
1960s? Every summer during those years I took my four children
camping up in the Keweenaw Peninsula. When we had to cope with
rainy days, playing Monopoly, going to the laundromat in Calumet,
or getting a sandwich in Laurium was something to do.

These nonidentical twin towns, joined at the intersection and
sharing the same mind-set, were strikingly charmless back then.
Old company-town houses with gray façades were lived in yet they
looked empty. The red sandstone structures of earlier years had
too many boarded-up windows; too many of the clustered churches
(once independent spirits) had closed doors. Anything resembling
real bustle was confined to two business blocks on Fifth Street in
Calumet. More than once the whole area was referred to as Michigan's Appalachia, scenic but dirt poor.

Now Calumet and Laurium are being rediscovered. Their
fabulously rich histories slowly are being recognized as a vital
corner of Americana that never made it into the national legends
the way gold-rush tales of California and silver fables of Colorado
did. They are now part of America's newest national site, the
Keweenaw National Historic Park, encompassing Calumet, Laurium,
and the Quincy Mine.

And their faces have brightened up considerably. A new

breed is repopulating the area: professors from the university in Houghton, grandchildren of old "Yupers," and retirees from southern cities. "Like living in a time warp," says one former Chicagoan; the present tense without the present tension.

The Calumet-Laurium story started when copper was found in deep, full veins, just beneath Keweenaw's rugged surface, sometimes pure enough to be used without refining.

The early 1840s saw America's first big mining rush. Thousands of prospectors, miners, traders, and hopefuls poured into the area, working against cold, black flies, and bleak conditions either individually or by hiring on with a mining company. The biggest and most successful (and politically powerful) company of all was the Calumet & Hecla firm, a Boston syndicate.

When a mine shaft was opened, the nearby workers' settlement was given the mine's name, so Calumet began as Red Jacket. Of course the con men, gamblers, saloon operators, and shady ladies came, too. After a hell-bent beginning known for hard-driving sin, Calumet's name was changed and things became respectable . . . and ethnically about as diverse as a town could get.

The expanding Calumet & Hecla (C & H) enterprise recruited miners in Europe, pulling the young and able-bodied from Cornwall, Croatia, Italy, Sweden, Estonia, Finland, Ireland, etc. They lived in company houses, bought from company stores, and worshipped in their own churches (partly paid for by the company and often very beautiful).

Calumet's population was largely labor; upper-crust mine managers and owners built elegant homes in Laurium, where the noise level was lower. Laurium had its rough side, however, but in the new historic park home-tour guide mostly mansions are pointed out.

To say C & H prospered hardly hints at the truth. In 1900 Calumet bragged of amenities like paved streets, trolleys, electric lights, buildings four floors high, plus five dozen saloons.

Looking for new places to spend money, Calumet lavished $70,000 on the first municipally owned opera house (the Calumet Theater) in the U.S. Jenny Lind sang here, Sarah Bernhardt emoted, and Enrico Caruso packed them in, 1,200 at a time. (John Philip Sousa, Lillian Russell, Otis Skinner, Houdini . . .)

Although accused of sharp practices and beset by periodic strikes, C & H built one of the best school systems of the era, put up a hospital with the newest technology, and erected a large modern library. Calumet and Laurium were good places to live; in fact much serious consideration was given to making Calumet the state capital.

The Keweenaw Peninsula's solid rock underpinnings contain hundreds of miles of mine tunnels. Nothing shows the impact of this operation quite like the C & H record book: more than two million tons of copper in the company's 100-year life, 6,000 employees who worked three shifts in the world's deepest mine shafts. At 6,000 feet, one shaft was deeper than six stacked World Trade Centers. (It also leaked acid water that blistered hands and destroyed clothing.) Sixty-three percent of the copper mined in the U.S. once came from C & H; investors earned $10 million in 1899; stock rose to $1,000 per share. The ravenous need for copper telegraph and telephone wires, electric motors, etc., seemed to insure the future.

It didn't. High-grade copper played out, the demand slackened with radio and new technology, the market price dropped, and the Great Depression hit. Calumet went from a city of 47,000 down to the edge of oblivion. Clustered spires of empty churches, boards over the opera house windows, weeds in the park gave forlorn testimony to times come and gone.

Hanging in there by a thread, however, were Calumet and Laurium, natives and alumnae, drawn back for family reunions and general love of the area.

In a resurgence of community life, interested groups saw to it that the theater was fully restored. It's a cream and gold beauty. Traveling dance troupes, even the Detroit Symphony Orchestra has played on its refurbished sixty-foot stage. You can join a tour group and visit the high balcony and backstage dressing rooms or sit in a box seat and imagine how it used to be. Call 906-337-2610 for information.

Calumet and Laurium: Sister Act

Hike around a few blocks. There is something about the stoic red sandstone buildings and simple shops that's like going back to

The Calumet Theater

11

the early 1940s or 1950s. In Thurner's Bakery on Fifth Street, simple breads and pies priced to compete with home kitchens are basic necessities for picnics. At Fifth and Portland streets are a couple of copper-art stores. Watch the process of heating copper "leaves" to bring out special color in artwork. Big selection, but alas, the raw red metal has to be purchased in Chicago from a wholesaler.

On Red Jacket Road the Copper Town Museum fills in a few gaps with pictures of grim-faced miners, information on the stamping mill process, drills, lamps, and tools from a tough trade. Call 906-337-4354. (You may learn more at the Michigan State History Museum, in Lansing, where the finely tuned exhibit on copper mining is a real winner.)

It won't mean a whole lot to the current generation of football fans, but their grandparents will remember "One for the Gipper," meaning George Gipp, the famous Notre Dame player who was a Laurium citizen. The house where he was born is attraction "A" on a self-guided walking tour list (it goes down to "O") of Laurium's historic residential district.

Star of the show is the Laurium Manor Inn, a bed and breakfast that was home-sweet-forty-room-home to Captain Thomas Hoatson, founder of another mining company. Features of the antebellum beauty include a third-floor ballroom, elephant-hide wall covering in the dining room (killing elephants for wallpaper didn't seem too outrageous in 1905). A mirror covers the entire back wall of the large entrance hall; the stairway windows are stained glass, and the fireplaces carved oak. The captain didn't miss a refinement, including a turntable in the carriage house so that a vehicle driven in wouldn't have to be backed out.

Neither have the current owners/innkeepers, Dave and Julie Sprenger. If it's impossible to spend the night (and snuggle under one of the handmade flannel quilts), at least take a house tour, offered daily at 1:00 P.M. for a small fee. The inn is located at 320 Tamarack Street; 906-337-2549.

The Laurium Manor Inn is the only house on the walking tour that you can enter. Others built by heavy-equipment makers,

superintendents, and one gentleman who doubled his mining fortune by opening a large department store in Laurium, are fun to
gaze at from the outside. Victorian verandas, corner windows,
etc., all seem solid and heavy, as befits homes in a climate that
brings down 200 to 300 inches of snow every winter.

Laurium has a small band shell where summer concerts are
held on Thursday evenings. Tune up by having a sundae at the
Honey Cone, located on Helca Avenue at Depot Street.

East on Lake Linden Street (State 26), a scenic slope down
to the village of the same name, takes you to the scene of old C & H
stamping mills where the company crushed rocks and floated the
copper out after the pure veins of metal thinned away. It also takes
you to a marvelous old-fashioned candymaker in the Lindell Chocolate Shoppe at 300 Calumet Avenue, where the rich chocolates are
hand-dipped, and where you can order ice cream too. Indulge.

The Houghton County Historical Museum, once a main mill
office, is now crammed with 10,000 items. Early washers, post
office items, bridal gowns, miner buckets, school clocks, and a picture of a nine-foot former citizen of Laurium are just some of the
pieces on display. For the dedicated seeker of memorabilia, call
906-296-0165 for visiting hours.

Meanwhile, back up on US 41, just a little north of the Calumet-Laurium juncture, two favorite eating places cannot be missed.
One is the Hut, in Kearsarge, a low-slung dimly lit and oddly
romantic place where the food is excellent and servings are lavish.
(Great lasagna.) Call 906-337-2122. Slightly beyond, on the same
side of the road, The Old Country Haus has log-cabin hominess
complete with a German heritage of great soups, a wide variety of
salads, and tempting desserts. Call 906-337-4626. (No breakfast is
served.)

On the way back down the peninsula, stop to stare at the
Quincy Mine shaft house—which maybe caused you to put on the
brakes on your way up. The hoist in the building next to it was
designed to haul men and machinery a distance of over one and a
half miles, and to carry ten tons of ore at a time at thirty-six miles
per hour. The strength required of the hoist and the nerveless

psyches of the miners involved can hardly be fathomed. Eventually open-pit mining in other parts of the country proved more profitable, but this has to be one of the wonders of the engineering world, akin to building a pyramid or the Golden Gate Bridge. A scale model of the steam hoist and a short film are open mid-June to Labor Day. Seeing the faces of men on their way deep into the hot, dangerous earth to earn a living should make anybody more grateful for their own job. Back outside, you are on the crest of a glorious hill with a view of forever. Praise be.

Keweenaw Tourism Council (Houghton): 906-482-2388;
   800-338-7982

3

Chelsea:
A Coveted Peace

". . . one night when the late train made its quick stop the rascals tied a stout rope around the station, tied the other end to the caboose, then watched gleefully as the flimsy building was dragged to smithereens. . . ."

In the 1800s there seemed to have been considerable more tolerance of high jinks than we'd allow today; this was the second station destroyed by pranksters. (The first time they lit a fire.) However, the Michigan Central Railroad responded with rare good temper to this vandalism by building a sturdy and really elegant little wooden station that stands between the tracks and the feed store. The train doesn't stop here anymore (you go to Ann Arbor to catch Amtrak), and the quaint depot is now the Chelsea Historical Museum.

That's the only kind of progress Chelsea really wants. Citizens watch uncomfortably as populations of other places look upon their town as a made-for-them suburb. Being close to Ann Arbor and the University of Michigan, not far from Lansing and Michigan State University, only thirty-eight miles from Detroit, part of a Michigan high-tech corridor, it's hard to stay an unspoiled country village with burgeoning populations closing in and licking their chops over you.

No getting around it, Chelsea is a neat little town. Leaving

I-94 at the Chelsea exit will bring you right onto Main Street. In three or four blocks tall trees and unpretentious old houses have set the atmosphere. The most conspicuous landmark looming just beyond the shops and cafés is a European-style clock tower of mixed architectural heritage. Since the building it graces is next to the railroad tracks, you can rightly suppose there is an industrial story behind it. Stoves were once made in this former foundry, now a warren of smaller business ventures.

Officially, Chelsea dates from 1834, when Sylvan Township was organized by local property owners living close to a spot where the Flint-Manchester road (dirt trail) crossed the Michigan Central tracks. What they really wanted was a local post office; solidifying into village status was the way to get one. By 1853 a gristmill had been built and the population leaped up to a robust sixty-three. At that time it was called Kedron, a name that didn't seem to sit well and "Chelsea" was voted in.

The hill that slopes down to the rail tracks and gives Chelsea a certain rolling ambience was a definite problem in early years. Even though it was on a main trail, this incline was one of the biggest sand mounds in the region. Drivers of freight wagons had to unload half their freight at the foot of the hill, unload the other half at the top while their horses rested, and return to the bottom for the first half. It's a wonder the whole town didn't move to Dexter.

Shovelful by shovelful the hill was leveled, the road improved, and progress made . . . slowly. It was 1911 before pennypinchers in the town council gave consent and splurged thirty-two cents apiece for street signs.

Like most towns the first products came from a blacksmith's forge or the barrelmaker's shop; beyond that Chelsea's first manufactured goods in 1852 were coffins, those somber necessities of life. Later came Welch and Hollier automobiles, paper, motorcycles, auto bumpers, flags, cement, books; Chelsea residents have had a hand in the whole nine yards. Publishing, machine parts, livestock feed, a Chrysler proving ground, and Jiffy Mixes—among others— keep the current economy stirring.

Among the short-lived enterprises of Chelsea was the Glazier

Stove Company which lasted only sixteen years but permanently affected Chelsea's profile. The towered factory beside the tracks is one reminder. An elegant English Gothic building next door represents an attempt on the part of Frank Glazier to keep his employees loyal. Called the "Welfare Building," it featured an indoor swimming pool, billiard hall, basketball court, theater, and reading room.

Built in 1906, the classy labor club was a little too much for Glazier's bookkeeping. He had to declare bankruptcy in 1907, only a year later. Since then, the faded ladylike structure has been home to the Chelsea and Dexter newspapers, and is now an official historic site.

As you explore Chelsea, a tour of the Chelsea Milling Company (those quick mixes) is fun and available to groups. If you're traveling as a couple, call ahead to see if a group is scheduled and see if you can join it: 313-475-1361.

Up and down North Main (State 52) are all the boutiques and interesting shops a browsing shopper could want. Around in back of the east side of the street (between East Middle and Park) is parking and a lively farmers' market, going strong on Saturdays between 8:00 A.M. and 1:00 P.M. until winter shuts it down.

Chelsea is blessed—if that's the word—with the usual fast-food emporiums on the edge of town, but for sturdier fare, the Common Grill was described by one writer as a good reason for going to Chelsea. She was absolutely right. Also on Main between Middle and Park, the Common is large, airy, and imaginative with a deep bow to Chelsea's past. A large mural shows the rooftops of the old town; blackboards proclaim the day's specialties. Try the three-onion soup or potato-crusted whitefish. No reservations needed but a call (313-475-0470) may save you a long wait on Saturday night.

Another big Chelsea draw is the Purple Rose Theater at 137 Park Street, a professional nonprofit showcase for Michigan talent featuring small, almost in-the-round intimacy and happily low prices. To find out what's coming, call 313-475-7902 for information. Tickets go on sale a month before stage time, costing $10 for previews, $14.00 to $18.00 for other times, and more for opening nights. *National Anthems* and *Possessed, the Dracula Musical*, summer productions in 1992, were described to me as great fun. Certainly something to look into.

On residential streets the long popularity of Greek Revival architecture is clear, supposing to have reflected America's admiration for the virtues of ancient Athens. A Chelsea Village tour

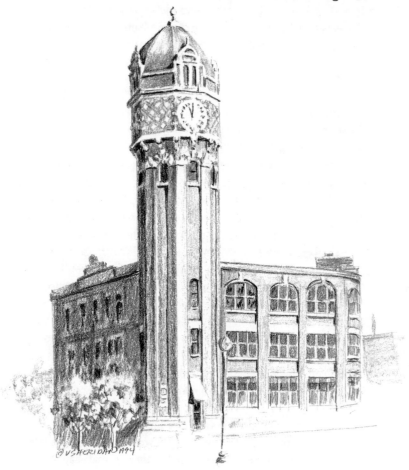

The old Chelsea clock tower

pamphlet is available on the first floor of the Sylvan Building, at the corner of Main and Jackson streets.

Another brochure called "Valleys and Vistas" puts you behind the wheel for a countryside excursion that begins at the clock tower and ends at the Methodist Retirement Home. In between you visit the Waterloo Recreation Area, a Centennial Farm, the Waterloo Farm Museum, and interesting remnants of the past—a schoolhouse, an old farm, barns, and cemeteries. Stop or don't stop, this makes a great color tour at the right time of year.

Chelsea Chamber of Commerce: 313-475-1145

4

Chesaning: Their Act Is Together

Bobby Vinton in Chesaning? Tennessee Ernie Ford? Steve Allen and Jayne Meadows? There's not a big theater or major soundstage in sight, but modest little Chesaning (population 2,567) has come up with a classic community event that brings in big names and thousands of visitors during one spectacular week in July.

Seven times in seven days, a showboat—paddle wheel, fluted smokestacks, and all—leaves its berth near the visitors center on State 57 and puffs down the Shiawassee River half a mile to a bandstand in Showboat Park. Bedecked with fancy lights and swirls of bunting, carrying big stars and a troupe of gifted amateurs, the vessel makes its grand entrance—a cue for wild cheers. Jamming bleachers and lawns, the audience is keyed for high-glitz musical fun. (Marie Osmond? Donald O'Connor? Pat Paulson . . . !)

This has been going on for more than fifty years.

Showbiz on a cast-of-hundreds scale would seem unlikely to succeed in Chesaning, a *small*, small town given to chicken dinners and antique auctions. In south central Saginaw County, Chesaning's forte is as a farm community, although lumber was big in its founding.

East-westbound State 57 becomes Broad Street, Chesaning's main downtown thoroughfare for five or six blocks on the east side. Ben Franklin Store, Country Charm Café, Malt Shop, family businesses are all there. A former village baptist church lives again as "Heavenly Creations," a gift shop with angel figurines, handmade quilts, etc.

Chat around. The question, Are you involved in Showboat Week? soon sounds silly. For starters, all the merchants are putting on a big sidewalk sale as showgoers explore town. When not actively on the job or in school, everyone seems to be in on the act and has been for most of their lives. An all-volunteer staff sells tickets, hands out programs, cleans bleachers, sews costumes, decorates the town. No one is shy in telling how they played a banjo, sang with the Endmen, or had a daughter who was second-runner-up for Queen.

Boy Scouts pop popcorn, the American Legion rents seat cushions; Odd Fellows and Rebekkahs run food booths, Methodist and Catholics plunge into providing Showboat dinners.

Not only is the whole town in on the act, the feeling grows that everyone is aunt, cousin, in-law, or otherwise kin to everyone else.

On the west end of Chesaning, Broad Street widens into a boulevard of grand old family houses recycled into gift boutiques with names like "Carousel," "Goody Closet," "Truly Scrumptious," or "Fancy That" and filled with old glass, hand-dipped candles, or collector toys.

Note the historic clock that once graced a downtown corner bank. After being taken down in 1966, community volunteers restored the works and put it to new use as a boulevard centerpiece.

A dandy sampler of 1895 architectural whimsies stands on the corner of Broad Street and Line. The Carousel (Stewart home) uses a round lattice of gingerbread to frame a front window; it has a tower with a high cone roof and little upstairs porches and dormers. (Great possibilities for hide-and-seek!) Inside (not too surprisingly) the Carousel Museum displays a collection of teddy bears among its other treasures (517-845-7881).

The eye-catching Heritage House is Chesaning's other claim to fame. A Georgian beauty with tall pillars and wide *porte cochere* (think *Gone With the Wind*'s "Tara" on a smaller lot), Heritage House is easily among the classiest restaurants in the state. Lumber baron George Nasson built the house as his family home in 1908; the Howard and Bonnie Ebenhoeh clan now run a dining business here with the energy and hospitality of the Brady Bunch.

Service spreads through seven rooms, from sedate to slightly more relaxed, but all of them inviting. Even the blue plush Louis XV chairs near the handcarved fireplaces or the rose carpeting are less formal than they sound. If you aren't seated there, at least peek into the upstairs Rose Room.

Edwardian helpings of roast duckling or pork tenderloin; big *big* servings of dessert. At Christmas the house is decorated from Rathskellar Bar to gift shop with thousands of lights for a fairy-tale glow. Reservations are recommended; during Showboat Week they are absolutely required. Telephone 517-845-7700.

The Heritage House owners also run the Bonnymill Inn (almost across the street), built from a 1920 farmer's grain mill and converted into a Victorian bed and breakfast. Some rooms have luxuries good Queen Vicky never heard of (Jacuzzi, wet bars) but the hot buffet breakfast is a timeless commodity.

North and south of Broad Street are the shady blocks that turn small towns into havens. The Chesaning Area Museum is on one such street, two blocks north of the Bonnymill Inn. The museum is not always open, so call ahead; 517-845-3055.

There's fast food and more places to eat where the boulevard gets back to two lanes west of Showboat Auto Sales. Or go back downtown to the Showboat Restaurant.

(Phyllis Diller? Pat Boone? Here?) The smiling hostess at the visitors center is glad to hand out literature telling the whole story. Credit is given to Chester M. Howell, owner and editor of the *Chesaning Argus*, for coming up with the idea. The town had a river, the river had a bend in it, and "showboats coming 'round the bend" had great appeal. Showboats had worked other places; why not here?

It took several years to sell the scheme, but when Harley Peet, of the Peet Packing Company, added $400 to the chamber

Chesaning's showboat

of commerce kitty (a whopping $100) there was no way to refuse.

First a dock and stage were erected in the park, then a boat was built by the owner of the Swartzmiller Lumber Company. He had never built a boat before so you might expect a few flaws in the design. As the opening-night boat pulled up to the park under spotlights and waving flags the cast of one hundred got wet feet standing on one side waving to the audience.

Bleachers were borrowed, the high-school band played, and a dancing quartet sent by the warden of the Ionia Reformatory was part of the talent show. It rained that week and the whole project lost money, but optimists pointed out that the audience was delighted.

In the course of two generations there isn't a phase of the show that hasn't gone back to the drawing board, been upgraded, sharpened, expanded, and timed. Today's fast-paced revue has felt the touch of experts, and after all these years the supporting cast of Chesaning citizens knows exactly what they're doing—especially those snazzy Bohaty dancing girls high stepping in their feathered plumes just like their counterparts in Las Vegas.

Best of all, with all the thousands of hours of volunteer help, the Showboat makes enviable amounts of money. Profits have helped to build a community swimming pool, expanded the public library, bought a new pumper and computer for the Chesaning Fire Department.

Even so it's not the only game in town. Chesaning puts on a big annual Classic and Antique Car Show on the Saturday of Memorial weekend. Beneath the tall trees of Showboat Park nearly a thousand classic cars polished to a glassy finish go on display. The day includes a swap meet, antique fire engines, and an oldies rock and roll session. (*Oldies rock and roll!* Take that, Grandpa. It puts Tommy Dorsey out of sight.)

An eighteen-hole golf course, a small airport with two 2,000-foot runways, big-time discount shopping just east at Birch Run; with all this Chesaning manages diversity along with its dominant showbiz theme.

Chesaning: Their Act Is Together

In August the wheels start paddling toward next year's performances and lining up assignments. (Pat Boone? Rich Little? Norm Crosby!) It's a happy tiger that Chesaning citizens have by the tail and no one is about to let go.

Chesaning Chamber of Commerce: 517-845-3055

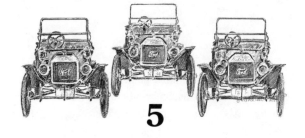

5

Colon: Now
Watch Closely...

Hidden up the long sleeve of a country road, the southern Michigan village of Colon goes through its year with little fanfare. School teams are cheered, Kiwanis and Lions, American Legion and Eastern Star have their meetings. There's a big Easter Egg Hunt and a parade on the Fourth of July.

In August, however, life in Colon takes a mildly bizarre turn when, "Presto!", Colon's modest population count of 1,245 leaps like a rabbit out of a top hat. Blame it on 1,000 magicians, merchants of illusion, who levitate in from around the world, filling motels, campgrounds, and every spare bedroom in St. Joseph County.

Some travel with pert assistants (leggy blondes preferred), most with smiley, patient wives who have gotten to know each other. A few tote odd luggage: cages of purple birds or folded display cases marked with old Mandrake stickers. These persons will be stars of evening shows, salesmen for tricky decks of cards and mysterious boxes, or they'll be giving how-to lectures.

Flexing their fingers in Olympic displays of manual dexterity, white-haired impresarios and ponytailed Houdinis huddle on porches or lawns discussing the good old days with glazed eyes, but they become as intense as lasers when watching a new stunt.

Such goings-on attract a following. Five to six thousand

simpler folk, good at gasping and applauding, also come to town for ticketed public events in the high-school gym.

The annual four-day Magic Get-Together, a fifty-year-old wingding, is sponsored by Abbott's Magic Company, maker of magician's supplies (flowers that pop from hats, ropes that stiffen in the air), and Colon's Lions Club.

The event draws some of the biggest names in hocus-pocus, each with a carefully cultivated specialty. Jeff McBride dazzles with now-you-see-him, now-you-don't entrances and exits; Bob Jepson throws his voice around; Amos Levkovitch proofs away white doves (and has often performed in Hollywood). The list reads like a sleight-of-hand *Who's Who*, if you know what's what.

Colon seems an unlikely Mecca for wizards. In breezily untheatrical farm country, it speaks plain talk, straight on. Midtown is thirty seconds from the village limits, where prim buildings have lined up to sell clothing, hardware, or antiques on State Street (State 87) for a century. There are two banks and three noteworthy places to eat. In Sedy's you can ponder a choice from thirty-seven kinds of sandwiches. Curly's Pool Parlor and the Five Star Pizza specialize in swift if not gourmet fixes. To work the only automatic teller machine in town you have to pretend to be a car, but a clear scarcity of traffic offers no threat.

At 219 Blackstone the Community Historical Society Museum fills an elderly house plus the small church next door. A huge clock makes it easy to find. Everybody over forty will recognize things they grew up with or saw at Grandma's, except for the magic memorabilia.

In a small but stately public library of mixed Beaux-Arts Italianate design (at 128 South Blackstone) an impressive near-million volumes is available to readers through a regional cooperative while 6,000 books line the shelves.

Half the streets of Colon are only a block long; beneath canopies of tall trees slow-track backyard living is alive and well, inviting enough to want to hang around and maybe even move in.

That must be how Mrs. Harry Blackstone, Sr., felt seventy years ago when her husband, the famous vaudeville magician, sent her off in the family car to find a place that was cool and had good fishing. Harry needed a spot where he and his troupe could spend summer months perfecting acts while having some semblance of a holiday.

He bought property still known as Blackstone's Island, and—quite naturally—going to watch this amazing new neighbor became a summer highlight for local residents.

One of Blackstone's visitors was old friend Percy Abbott, another performer and builder of illusion props. The two of them formed the business which now bears Abbott's name. Unhappily, a feud broke up the friendship even as the business flourished.

The number of travelers who drop in to the Colon library may be low, but no one comes to this village without visiting Abbott's Magic Company, a few feet south of State Street on St. Joseph Avenue. Nothing too enchanting about the looks of this plain flat-top cement-block building painted black. It would have had a slightly spooky look even without the pair of skeleton murals.

Go in past the front desk to the salesroom and mini-auditorium to explore. There is something slightly musty about the atmosphere, as though you are entering a large secret closet. Maybe it's the lack of windows.

The low ceiling is invisible behind a patchwork of yellowed theatrical posters advertising magic shows of bygone days (a real item, that ceiling!). Along the walls old-time display cases hold samples of the stock, but one side of the room has a small stage. Sturdily built bleachers fill most of the floor space, providing room for an audience of seventy-five—more or less. (Shows at 1:00 P.M. and 3:00 P.M. on Saturdays from Memorial to Labor Day are pass-the-hat affairs but it is suggested that $3.00 is a fair sum.)

At the counter the jovial present owners demonstrate entry-level gimmicks (boxes that seem to make a coin vanish, etc.) to intrigued tourists. Or you can cull through racks of how-to booklets: "Tokyo Magic," "Tearing Gospel Lessons," "Newspaper Magic," "Self-Working Card Tricks," "Tricks for Birds," "Animal Tricks," etc. Might give a person a whole new professional goal.

When the big August weekend arrives, magic takes over the

high school. Former classrooms are transformed into magic merchandise marts, areas closed to the general public. Lab counters, art tables, and bulletin boards are draped with lures from the inventive minds of a peculiar business. The pros sort through the latest in scarves that open into fifty-foot ropes or interlocking metal

Enjoy some magic

hoops as though they were miners at a dig. They confer over coffee sold by the Colon parents' group; greet acquaintances with boisterous cries that drown out rivalry for the time being.

Outside, Colon citizens seize a chance to have sidewalk sales and garage sales, run pop stands, sell cookies. Churches may put on a fund-raising supper or pancake breakfast. For antique collectors, the pickings are ripe.

A few that do not go along with the fun are the Amish and Mennonite families in the surrounding farm area. Any other day you may meet an Amish buggy on the road or see one parked in the village while its owner takes care of a little business. However, to them all foolery is devilish, and the sooner back to the farm the better.

St. Joseph County, on the Indiana border, is blessed with a dozen little lakes, two of them within Colon township. Palmer Lake provides sixteen miles of shore around its 450 acres, enough for waterskiing or just taking the old innertube cool-off treatment. When the scene turns to ice, there's plenty of ice fishing, skating, snowmobiling, and even a Swiss-type lodge for cross-country skiers.

In fall, the maples and elms put on a colorful show of their own; a great time to mosey out Ralston Lake Road for excellent country dining at the cozy River Lake Inn. Get exact directions when making reservations; telephone 616-432-2626.

Housekeeping cottages may be available at the Palmer Lake Lodge and Bait Shop (616-432-3404) but best bets for housing are in Coldwater or Three Rivers, and Kalamazoo is under forty miles away. Seekers of the supreme bed-and-breakfast experience should try for the sumptuous Georgian colonial Chicago Inn on US 12 in Coldwater. More information is available from the West Michigan Tourist Association (616-456-8557).

I had time before leaving Colon to try a Sedy's Rueben sandwich and thumb through the newest copy of *Tops*, a magazine for magicians published by Abbott's. Full of descriptions of card tricks, etc., it also contained a riveting ad for "Magicraft's Visible Sawing Thru." Get this: "Now you can perform the famous Sawing a Girl in Half in a neat portable method using a real power saw. Borrow a girl from the audience, place her on any table, and cover her middle with the wooden frame. The power jigsaw runs through the frame, apparently right through the girl's body. Imagine the excitement of this thrilling effect . . . Can be performed anywhere without fear. The girl herself has no idea as to how the trick works. A feature effect for any act and at a great price too! ($180)"

Well, no one is going to saw *this* girl without fear!

I went back to Abbott's, bought a pierce-the-coin trick, and left town.

The name Colon (which leaves much to be desired if you are medically minded) was derived from the punctuation mark. To quote from an old letter, "Arrangements were made and a surveyor laid out the lots. When completed we wished to give it a name . . . could not find one to suit. Finally, I took up an old dictionary and the first word I put my hand on was 'colon.' Looking to see the definition . . . a mark of punctuation indicating a pause almost as long as that of a period, we called it 'Colon'."

West Michigan Tourist Association: 616-456-8557

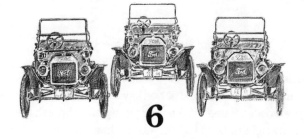

6

Crystal Falls:
Will of Iron

I have never seen a parade in Crystal Falls, one of the rare places still celebrating Victory Over Japan Day, but I am sure that all marching is done away *from* the courthouse, not *toward* it.

The big redstone Romanesque structure with a clock in its lookout tower and mysterious narrow windows in a small second tower sits like an old emperor on the crest of a slope that would do credit to San Francisco. Its imposing entrance faces Superior Avenue, the main business thoroughfare (US 2), which will strike visitors as suitable for downhill skiing.

On the Fourth of July, V-J Day, or whatever, processions start at the high school in back of the court, high-step around to the front, and head downhill; the queen's car in low gear, the band leaning stiffly backwards. Especially drummers who must cope with extra forward ballast.

Crystal Falls is a town that likes things a little tough. Deeply embedded in the western Upper Peninsula, near Wisconsin's border and away from big lakes, the countryside surrounding Crystal Falls rises and dips in pine-green vistas, rugged edges, and memories of iron. Forget chic boutiques and pricey dining; think fishing, hearty home meals, tire chains, fleece-lined jackets, and an all-seasons outdoor life.

Crystal Falls: Will of Iron

The community had its start in 1846 when William Burt's survey crews noticed their compasses acting up. By 1851 the cause was pinned down by land surveyor Harvey Mellen's find of an "outcropping of iron ore five feet high."

Mellen and Burt had discovered the rich western end of a whopping lode of pay rock that became know as the Menominee Range. (Iron ore was found in areas called "ranges." The Marquette and Gogebic ranges were two others in upper Michigan.)

German immigrant George Runkel came early on the scene and organized the Crystal Falls Iron Company, named for a white-water stretch on the Paint River.

A settlement begun by Runkel and his ilk flourished. They acquired a post office, saloons, and political clout, especially when it became clear that Crystal Falls was developing a larger number of mines in the immediate vicinity than any other Upper Peninsula town. Railroads soon made it easier to ship ore; mining boomed.

So did an intense rivalry with Iron River, slightly to the west. When Iron County was first organized by the state legislature, Iron River was named as temporary county seat until a citizens' vote could decide the matter.

Crystal Falls wanted badly to be the town where people came to register deeds, probate wills, get a marriage license. Since people taking care of such matters left cash with local merchants, being designated county seat ranked high on a town's political wish list.

Impatient and sure that the slow-moving referendum was endangering their chances, a few Crystal Falls residents fell to plotting a solution in the best spy-novel tradition. Their object: steal the county records.

(Fact and legend get a little muddled here.) As the story goes, a poker game was arranged right after a county commissioners' meeting in Iron River. When sufficient time went by, two Crystal Falls boys pretended to quit and go to bed. Instead they sneaked over to the temporary courthouse (with some conniving confederates), packed the county papers on a sled to take to the depot, and put it all into a boxcar headed for Crystal Falls. The whistle blew as the train pulled out; unaware Iron River players kept dealing out cards.

On home ground the thieves hid everything in a mine shaft.

When Iron River citizens woke up to what had happened, they were livid. War nearly broke out, but residents followed the legislature's orders to call for a vote . . . or at least the appearance of a vote. Both sides pulled sly tricks such as registering dead men, bringing in lumberjacks from other counties to cast ballots, and tearing up opposition ballots. By a margin of five extremely doubtful votes, Crystal Falls became the new county seat.

The heat of the long-gone battle can still be felt today in an unusually fierce rivalry between the two towns. Now and then someone from Iron River will suggest a new vote on the matter. It was five years, however, before Crystal Falls was allowed to get started on its courthouse. That was 1884.

Mining is finished. Part of Iron County's underpinnings lives on in the steel framework of the nation's skyscrapers. Over a century, more than 250 *million* tons of iron ore came from this region, a task bringing in hundreds of Finnish, Scandinavian, and Italian immigrants. Today's phone books reflect this mixed heritage, as does the regional accent, "Yuper" talk. (If yer from da U.P., honk, eh?)

Sit down on a bench in front of Rosie's (about halfway to the top of the hill on Superior Street) with an ice cream cone from her selection of Mackinac Island ice cream, apple pie ice cream, peanut butter ripple, and then gaze around.

Except for its slant and a grand view to the east, the street is like many main streets with a Ben Franklin store, office of the *Diamond Drill* newspaper, a bakery, hardware, clothing. There is a friendly café or two, public library, and one small movie house, the Crystal Theater, now recharging its batteries. A restored theater organ adds tempo to teen activities, plays, and an intermittent schedule of live entertainment. Telephone 906-875-4179.

Around the corner, a block north on Fourth Street and far from any sign of water, stands a large 1895 cement-block house built in "steamboat" architecture with wrap-around porches. It is the Crystal Falls Harbor House Heritage Center, i.e., historical museum. The name suggests a sailors' haven, but when former owner Miss Minno Harbor and her relatives moved in, the "Harbor" house it truly was.

You can take in a great view of the Paint River Valley from the porch; inside, visit rooms of Victorian bric-a-brac and period pieces. (No, don't try out the velvet fainting couch.) Upstairs bedrooms house special collections of Crystal Falls' sport trophies and military memorabilia. Call for a schedule of museum events or open hours; 906-875-4179.

In Caspian, about two miles south of Iron River, wander through the buildings of a former mine site, engine house, etc., and see models of mine shafts, "skips" hauling ore up, and the general anatomy of an iron mine plus the world's largest miniature logging camp. Cutting and hauling are part of the exhibit, of course, but also little tidbits of camp life are revealed, such as how the tough camp cook made sure eating time was not wasted by talking and stood by with a butcher knife to insure silence and speed.

Rag rugs made by Finnish women on home looms during the long winter months are part of the show. The on-site LeBlanc Art Gallery was named for a former Hollywood cartoonist who came back to his roots in Iron County, having won many prestigious awards for wildlife stamps and prints. Shows at the Caspian Iron Museum lean toward outdoor topics well selected. A gift shop has gifts unique to the Upper Peninsula. Open daily from June through August; shorter hours in May and September. On Museum Road; telephone 906-265-2617.

Iron County gets to work out on three "sporty" (their adjective) golf courses: the Crystal Falls Municipal Course, a half-mile east of town on State 669, and two others south of Iron River.

Try visiting Iron County during the Annual Bass Festival, when the true character of the county comes forward and is best described as friendly, informal, and more than a tad competitive.

Tell-it-like-it-is titles for events (the Wop-Swede softball game; the 10K Run Your Bass Off footrace) say it best. A parade on Saturday, marvelous chicken barbecue in Runkle Lake Park on Sunday, bands playing, bratwurst steaming, canoes racing . . . Every good thing about small towns comes alive during this event which takes place on the second weekend in July.

The V-J Day party is in August, the month of the County Fair over in Iron River. Year-round calendar events again favor fresh air; Humungus Fungus Festival (Sept.); bear, grouse, deer hunting seasons (fall); Snowmobile Poker Run (Feb.); cross-country and downhill skiing nearby at the Ski Brule Lodge, Iron River.

Two motels are listed in the Crystal Falls yellow pages; the Falls Motel on US 2 (906-875-3168), and the Four Seasons Motel on Crystal (906-875-6596); three others can be found in Iron River. The bed and breakfast idea has been a little slow to catch on around here, but there are plenty of resorts with cabins for one night or ten. You might want to call the chamber of commerce for suggestions or grab a phone book and look under "resorts" if you plan on visiting during a festival or hunting season. (Business is met with a certain casual indifference when the state says go ahead and shoot.)

They do a little better on the dining list. Expect wholesome hearty servings at the Lunchbox Deli, 700 Crystal, 906-875-6700; Memory Lane Resort Restaurant and Lounge, 798 US 141, 906-875-6949; or drive to Amasa up US 141 about eighteen miles for country talk and warm atmosphere at the Pine Cone Café; 906-822-7713.

Iron County had the first roadside table in the state, and therefore in the nation since Michigan was a pioneer in roadside facilities. At Bewabic State Park, just west of Crystal Falls, where picnic tables are as plentiful as fish stories, there are 144 campsites, in case you miss the motel, and great fishing opportunities if you like doing meals from scratch. For more campground information, call 906-875-3324.

Crystal Falls: Will of Iron

Crystal Falls has a mind of its own, and in these days of tight conformity, that's a fresh breeze from the north.

Crystal Falls Chamber of Commerce: 800-255-3602

7

Dowagiac: What's in a Name?

Boss McKee of the Michigan Central Railroad was dictating a letter addressed to his superintendent who was coming from Chicago to meet him. "Tell him," said McKee to his secretary, "to meet me in Dowagiac."

The secretary paused. "Mr. McKee, how do you spell 'Dowagiac'?"

McKee stared at her a moment. "Dowagiac? . . . Dowagiac? . . . Oh hell. Tell him to meet me in Niles!"

On the side of a furniture factory in town, a large logo shows an Indian and "Doe-Wah-Jack" written in plain syllables. The name is an Indian word said to mean "foraging around"; hardly spellable, barely pronounceable, yet somehow euphonic.

To those who know it best, Dowagiac means charm; a neat little city in green, lush Cass County, full of lakes and farms, apple orchards, wide fields of cucumbers, and bacon still on the hoof. From Dowagiac it only takes thirty minutes to reach Lake Michigan, two hours to get to either Detroit or Chicago via Amtrak. As I-94 slices across southwestern Michigan, it's just far enough north of town not to interfere with Dowagiac's air of genteel remoteness.

Remote does not equate with out-of-sync. Kurt Vonnegut visited and was impressed. John Updike and Joyce Carol Oates are among names found on Dowagiac calendars. The restoration-preservation factor is alive and well. A short stroll around the downtown business section quickly reaffirms Dowagiac's old-young mind-set.

Early town planners intended that Main Street, at right angles to the railroad tracks, be the commercial lane, but savvy merchants wanted sites as close as possible to the rail passenger trade, so shopping developed along Front Street (which parallels the tracks) instead.

Except for concrete pavement, updated traffic, and some imaginative paint jobs, Front Street looks pretty much the way it did when nineteenth-century folks got off the trains, including the antique-style streetlights.

Enthusiasm for Victorian embellishment hits a peak at Zeke's Restaurant and Bar where the colorful façade is painted in muted blue, purple, cream, pink, and green. Add lace curtains. This could be ghastly but every touch manages to hit the right note.

Nearby, Phillipson's turns out to be Michigan's oldest men's store, run by the same family since 1858.

Another survivor, Caruso's Candy Kitchen, has been stirring up luscious homemade chocolate, almond toffee, caramels, etc. (plus lunch), for three generations. Ice cream blow-outs come over an old-fashioned Italian soda fountain where the countertop is marble and a huge mirror forms the back bar. A tin ceiling and dark old display cases hint that Caruso's is just as it used to be, and no-body's about to change a thing.

In 1925 you could buy a sundae for ten cents, a combination lunch for a dime (soup and sandwich), coffee for a nickel. Unhappily, some changes can't be reversed.

Many of Front Street's 1800s buildings have oval bronze plaques on them, telling who the earlier owners were, what was sold, and who did the restoration. For example "Achie Fleming's Feed Store, restored by . . ."

Some sturdy iron and chrome parlor stoves of rather elegant trim were standing in store windows when I sauntered through.

They turned out to be from a private collection of Round Oak heaters, stoves, and furnaces—the Kenmores and General Electrics of their day and made in Dowagiac.

A block south of Front Street emporiums, the low-profile train station houses a secretary of state office. It's the kind of depot that miniaturizes into a great accessory for a train set. Deep overhanging eaves shelter anyone watching for Amtrak's Chicago- or Detroit-bound runs. In the waiting room are wooden benches of a past generation, but no ticket window; passengers are ticketed on board.

Across the tracks stretch the holdings of the Ameriwood Furniture Company, Dowagiac's biggest employer, and the Judd Lumber Company, the oldest continuously operated lumber business in the state.

Between City Hall's back door, a parking lot, and heavy bushes, the memorial to Dowagiac's Civil War heroes would not seem to get a lot of attention; perhaps the cannon-monument tribute to World War II dead, in the middle of a Main Street corner, does better.

Surface history. The deeper story of Dowagiac goes back to 1830 when William Renesten built a carding mill at the point where an old Indian trail between Kalamazoo and Niles crossed the "Da-wa-ga-awk River." Two years later the stalwart newcomer settler dammed the creek to create a millpond at the eastern end of town. In 1883, he built a gristmill, another man erected a sawmill, and with settlers coming around to look for jobs, the community seed had been planted. Today the Mennell Milling Company, formerly Colby Mills, is Michigan's oldest mill operating on its original site.

In 1848 the hamlet's entire population could still fit into four log houses when the Michigan Central Railroad decided to build a depot at this point, thus putting Dowagiac on the maps while spurring its growth as a livestock and grain shipping center.

Another route into town, the stagecoach between Niles and Kalamazoo, also brought land seekers and opportunists—whose thirsts required tending to, naturally. One of the first lucrative businesses was a tavern where the Village Market now stands. By

1900 there were ten saloons, down from a high count of sixteen. Whiskey sold for three cents a dipperful—and brought on a few brawling fatalities.

A snippy lady journalist visited Dowagiac in the early 1850s, reporting to her Philadelphia readers "there is not enough grass in Dowagiac to bleach a sheet on." Locally, that stung, but the comment spurred local interest in growing grass and making things look nice. Grander homes and wider lawns were on their way with the arrival of Philo Beckwith in 1854. Beckwith devised a drill that revolutionized the way small grain was planted, and he developed the Round Oak stove. Dowagiac prospered, became chic, and grew spreading lawns.

The first car, a seven horsepower Haynes-Apperson, arrived in town in 1899, bringing spectators from miles away. It was remembered that the car was "somewhat temperamental and frequently had to be hauled by a team of horses." Embarrassing, but it kindled sparks. With the means for metal works at hand, two auto companies were organized in 1908; the Lindsley Company and the Dowagiac Motor Car Company. The first put out fifteen cars (twelve horsepower, $250.00 list price) and went bankrupt. Two cars survive, one of them in the Auto Museum of Auburn, Indiana. The Dowagiac auto truck wagon had better luck until sold to a Tulsa, Oklahoma, firm where it sputtered to a dead end.

Other Dowagiac products include James Heddon's artificial fishing lures, an invention mothered directly by necessity. Heddon, up a creek with a pole and no lure, hastily whittled a wooden one that tempted a passing bass into taking its final bite. The lures of Heddon are used worldwide, although the business left Dowagiac in 1983.

King Gillette, inventor of the safety razor, spent some early years in Dowagiac, then headed east. Stoves, lures, etc., aside, it looked for a moment as though area fame would come from a totally different direction. Mother Nature held a dazzling prospect when Isaac Wells, Sr., digging gravel north of town, spotted something sparkling with an eerie brilliance. He took the pretty rock to a jeweler who declared it to be a diamond, later confirmed by the

"Made in Dowagiac"

Dowagiac: What's in a Name?

Smithsonian Institution in Washington. The jeweler bought the eleven-carat stone from Wells for $100.00, and told Wells to keep it a secret. Wells didn't tell but kept looking for others. None were found. Theory has it that this was a "loner" washed down from an undiscovered source somewhere in Canada. By the time the diamond secret was out, the gravel pit filled with water and now no one knew just where to look. The only diamond ever found in Michigan was cut up long ago and made into several rings.

Diamonds or no, industrious Dowagiac knew enough prosperity to erect some rather wondrous houses worth staring at. At 405 West High Street, a three-story mansion called "The Rockery" is built of stones—turret, coach entrance, and all. The Gardner home, another fieldstone dwelling, had a staircase so carefully crafted of bird's-eye maple that it was exhibited at the 1893 Columbia Exposition in Chicago.

Italianate, Queen Anne, Greek Revival houses can be found mostly on High, Main, Michigan, and Division streets. The oldest is an 1830 place at 302 West Telegraph. Note the front door and windows. Most interesting in some ways is the Victorian house built for John Lindsey: it weighs 110 tons. That's important to know because the house was moved—stained-glass windows, carved oak woodwork and all—from its site on Main Street to 208 Michigan Avenue; no small feat.

A self-guided walking tour booklet, "Visit Historic Dowagiac," is available to those who drop into the chamber of commerce office on Beeson Street. Then poke into the Southwestern Michigan College Museum. This branch of Michigan's community college network contains more bits and pieces of history, such as remembrances of Dowagiac's role in the Underground Railroad, Indian artifacts, settler's tools, oil cans, quill pens, and more stoves, in permanent and temporary exhibits. Light and optics, electricity, computers, hands-on displays—it's not just history any more but a handsome covering of several fields in displays popular enough to bring about a recent museum expansion. The museum is located at 58900 Cherry Grove Road; telephone 616-782-5113, extension 334.

After the Fourth of July, fireworks, and parade, the big fun event is the August Rod and Roll Auto Show & Flea Market which brings a gleaming line of classic old Reos and Packards and their next of kin into town, along with bargain hunters from all over. As the Dowagiac Art Guild is putting on its annual arts and crafts show at the same time, you can look for cookouts and dancing in the streets.

From May through October the Beckwith Theater Company goes into action with great talent; the Barn Swallow Theater is a June treat. Then think cold for an old-fashioned Christmas, open houses, caroling, and lights.

Up Indian Lake Road, Wick's Apple House sells more than apples, and cooks more than dinner on a 100-year-old family farm market which has been expanded into a bakery, cider mill, fruit market, and a delightful restaurant with a view of the orchard. Open Memorial Day through October; telephone 616-782-7306.

Back on Front Street you'll be suitably fed at the Round Oak Restaurant, Phreddie's Restaurant, or at Zeke's friendly tables.

But I have this awful sweet tooth and think a "King Tut" at Caruso's (two scoops ice cream, cherries, mixed nuts, sugar wafers . . .) is needed. Or maybe just a tuna on rye.

Spending the night is a little difficult, as no motels or bed and breakfasts are listed as of this writing in any of the tourist brochures regarding Dowagiac. However, you are near a Great Lake beach, near Niles, Coldwater, Kalamazoo, Benton Harbor, et al, and accommodations are close at hand.

Or call the Dowagiac Chamber of Commerce and see if they know of a spare room.

Dowagiac Chamber of Commerce: 616-782-8212

8

Gaylord:
Bring Your Clubs

It's hard to tell about a town if you don't get any closer than the gas and fast food at an Interstate exit. As I-75 zips its way north to the Mackinac Bridge and points beyond, Gaylord is a two-exit place, a map milestone telling you there are only sixty miles left in the lower peninsula.

The first exit is old US 27 (South Otsego Avenue) with motels, fuel, food, and a K Mart. The second exit, State 32 (West Main Street), has all the brand names you know by heart (McDonald's, Wendy's, Best Western) and shopping. Signs of a large community. State 32 also ties Charlevoix on Lake Michigan (forty miles west) to Alpena on Lake Huron (seventy-six miles east).

Good news: the real Gaylord is more than the sum of its exits, and much more than a busy crossroads. As a basically rural village with a year-round population of less than 1,500, Gaylord only stretches a dozen blocks east and west, fourteen blocks north and south. It is nevertheless big enough to serve as Otsego County seat, encompass the county fairgrounds, and play the role of hostess with the mostess in a vacation party land; resorts, skiing, hunting, camping, elk viewing, conventions, snowmobiles, canoeing, fishing, scenic bike routes. Add twenty-two golf courses (eighteen to forty-five holes with more on the drawing boards) within easy mileage of city hall. Gaylord's greens belt includes the thickest concentration of designer courses anywhere in the country (Robert Trent Jones, Sr., Tom Fazio, Al Watrous, and eight others). In and around Gaylord only deep snow and dark of night can keep the addict from his game.

The central miles of the northern lower Peninsula are a gentle rolling part of Michigan, once coldly covered with pine, tamarack, cedar, hemlock, and birch. In the 1800s the towering white pine was money pointing to the sky, and Gaylord (once called "Barnes") began in the usual Michigan town way: with a sawmill. An expanding America needed all the lumber it could get and with a seemingly unlimited supply thoughts of conservation just never occurred.

Until it was gone.

The last remaining stand of white pine today in all their stately magnificence can be seen in Hartwick Pines State Park and Lumber Museum, just east of I-75 between Gaylord and Grayling. Park rangers not only tell the hows and whats of logging, but the sometimes painful details of a worker's hard, cold, sweaty, underpaid, and underfed life . . . including the life that came to co-inhabit his long johns, insulation that seldom came off all winter. Gaylord's history is tightly laced into stories told at Hartwick Pines.

The Gaylord area population grew when Civil War veterans given homestead rights came up to clear land and start farms. Usually their long-suffering wives did the farming while the men brought in a smidgeon of extra funds as loggers.

It was 1875 when this mid-upstate region was officially organized into a county named Otsego, an Indian word meaning "beautiful lake." Nearby Otsego Lake was the one referred to, and for a while the county seat was a spot on its shores. When Gaylord took over as seat, a stately Romanesque county courthouse was built with a tall tower and all the embellishments a house of government was due.

As the century turned, Gaylord acquired a depot and scheduled train stops, as well as an assortment of businesses. For a while G. M. stood for Gaylord Motors as a local plant turned out utility vehicles for farms and truckers plus a few passenger cars. A lone survivor of this enterprise sits in the Gaylord-Otsego County Chamber of Commerce building at South Otsego and First streets, but proudly rolls down the street in special parades.

Another big business (with a longer life span) turned out practical items such as the wooden forms cobblers used in making shoes, wooden tenpins, and rough golf-club heads, selling them around the world.

Although golf was literally gaining ground, in the early 1900s baseball took the field. Listed among Gaylord's 1914 recreational diversions was a hometown ball team, the Otsegos, that toured the state with an enviable record. In twenty towns they suffered only two losses; one of them to the Detroit Tigers, who had the famous Georgia Peach, Ty Cobb, in their lineup.

World War I, the Depression, World War II. One positive blessing of the Depression of the early 1930s was the Civilian Conservation Corps, a works-project program that did much to restore the dwindling forests. Natural gas was discovered and has since become a source of regional income, while the business of tourism was mushrooming with better roads, faster cars, and a post-war generation who looked upon getting away from it all "up north" as more of a right than a privilege.

Catering to a transient population shakes today's Gaylord, where they decided in the mid-1960s to adopt the nickname "The Alpine Village" and redecorate the town accordingly. This may bemuse those who have seen a real Alp, but it works for Gaylord, a town that happens to sit on the highest point in southern Michigan, a modest 1,395 feet above sea level. (All rivers flow away from the city. The Sturgeon, Pigeon, and Black rivers flow north; Manistee and North Branch AuSable flow south).

Little balconies, window boxes, and painted flowers were added to buildings and homes. For its part, Glen's market on West Main installed a glockenspiel (mechanical clock) that plays on twenty bronze bells every fifteen minutes between 8:00 A.M. and 10:00 P.M. In nice weather two animated figures come out of little doors and wave. Sensors in their clockwork innards keep them warm and dry when storms blow in (Swiss-like attention to detail!).

Even though there were probably more Polish and German than Swiss settlers here, nobody much cares. During the third week in July the population happily dons dirndls and liederhosen to yodel, dance, and parade through an Alpenfest, convincing themselves and the world that if they weren't of Swiss descent they should have been. One feature of the fest, the world's biggest coffee break, is suspiciously all-American but a lot of international fun.

Gaylord even made a civic bond with Pontresia, Switzerland, sister city back "home."

The mood is Alpine but the feeling is down-home friendly. As you walk around town you won't see the old courthouse, replaced years ago by a newer structure with decidedly Swiss contours. The Otsego County Historical Museum, 320 West Main Street, will please old-timers and perhaps puzzle the young who can't imagine life before movies. On display are quilts, quills, and documents to pour over; telephone 517-732-6662. The Mount Carmel Center on North Otsego was for a long time one of the smallest cathedrals in the United States. These days it serves as a local theater and entertainment center. A few blocks south on the corner of Second Street the First Congregational Church has reached the status of a National Historic site.

Maybe too far from the town center for some of us to hike but only blocks away, the Call of the Wild Museum has been around for many years as an outstanding private enterprise. Well-done dioramas of Michigan animal life with taxidermied wolves, deer, rabbits, etc., are exhibited in realistic scenes. Follow paw prints through the museum, flip through the books and cards in the gift shop. The museum is at 850 South Wisconsin; telephone 517-732-4568.

Back in the center of town heavy knit Irish sweaters, the best in tailored suits, art goods and imports, handcarved wildlife sculptures, high-priced jewelry are all available; shopping is not just aimed at outfitting the guy in the duck blind.

This is easy to understand after you visit a few of the nearby golf-ski retreats, where in-room Jacuzzis are basic equipment and providing upscale luxuries for guests keeps the competition hopping.

It is the land of the spreading log and stone wide-lobby layout, with gourmet dining, convention meeting rooms, and kid-care nannies. Michaywe, 517-939-8911; Garland, 800-968-0042; Hidden Valley, 800-752-5510; Treetops, 800-444-6711.

The visitor may wonder where all the skiing takes place. The horizon holds secrets: valleys and dips make for fine scenic downhill slopes, such as those at Hidden Valley where the vertical drop at the Otsego Ski Club is 317 feet. Also, the hills of western Michigan (Boyne, Schuss, for example) are not far away.

I found glorious insinuations about Gaylord's true heritage subtly hidden in the pierogis, kielbasa, and kapusta of Busia's Polish Kitchen on Old 27 South, 517-732-2790. Same street, different kitchen, Mama Leone's Italian Restaurant can be found. If the food was more authentically Italian you'd come out with an accent.

Among the plenitude of other activities to be enjoyed, golf tourneys, bike marathons, and fishing derbies take up the Gaylord calendar. As of this writing the town is even planning its first (and hopefully annual) Float Plane Fly-In on Otsego Lake the second week in June.

Gaylord-Otsego County Chamber of Commerce: 517-732-4000; 800-345-8621 (out of state)

9

Grand Ledge: Cliff-Hanger

In late 1830 the Grand Ledge area was described as an "impenetrable forest." Sixty years later alarm was expressed over a growing traffic problem; twenty-seven sputtering, noisy automobiles were owned within the village limits.

Today Grand Ledge, within honking range of I-96 and minutes from downtown Lansing (about as accessible as a town can get), lives like the rest of us with traffic, and yet manages a quiet, almost secluded existence.

The ledges inspiring the name aren't an immediately visible attraction; they don't overlook the town like great background cliffs, but they are a deep river cut made eons ago through a much higher plain.

And they are lovely.

On the banks of the Grand River (one of Michigan's longest streams) where the present town stands, Indians from several tribes used to gather in spring and summer to tap maple trees for syrup, make pots from river clay, weave baskets from river grasses. Hunting and fishing together where bear, fox, and wild pigs roamed freely, several tribes shared this natural wild park. Famed Chief Okemos is buried not far away.

Slowly, without battle but with strange papers called property deeds, white settlers trickled in and another sad tale of Indian replacement began. By the 1840s there were six log houses on River Street; by 1850 they named their community Grand Ledge. Soon afterward they had a dam, sawmill, gristmill, foundry, and all the other makings of independence.

Plus a pair of colorful entrepreneurs. "Skink Skin John" (John Burtch) sold lumber and animal skins until he built a small sight-seeing boat and a resort house on Second Island.

J. C. Mudge, with the wheels spinning in his head, bought Burtch out in 1886, added a larger hotel, casino, dance pavilion, and even a Chinese pagoda and roller coaster.

Carried away, perhaps by his successes, Mudge made a real contribution to the annals of outlandish architecture by building a three-story round dwelling on the island. OK, but the three stories were all supposed to revolve slowly at different speeds. It didn't work. Ever.

The booming tourist trade was made even "better" when mineral wells were tapped. A trip to see the ledges was good for your health.

Trainloads of summer visitors came to picnic, ride the sight-seeing boats, sing, and have fun. The holiday heyday lasted forty years, but those worrisome automobiles turned out to be the big spoilers. People could get to new vacation spots without trains, and see things they hadn't seen before. Resort facilities went unused, were battered by floods, and finally torn down.

Islands, cliffs, and the village of Grand Ledge didn't exactly settle for obscurity, but they were dropped from the list of must-sees.

I reached the town near the end of the day, but decided to visit the ledges, starting in Fitzgerald Park. On the west side of Grand Ledge, Fitz Park is a generously spacious spread for a town of less than 7,000 with room enough in its seventy acres to boast a fish ladder, nature and cross-country ski trails, and even a summer theater. In Grand Ledge's era as a resort, the Spotlight Theatre was built to house the meetings of spiritualists; reports of haunting performances, however, have another meaning.

The "Ledges Trail," slightly above the banks of the river,

ambles between riverside trees and rock; a corridor in a cool, green twilight zone with walls of moss-coated sandstone ledges, sometimes boulderlike, often with strata randomly stacked as though done by an unsteady child. You can see the brownish river flowing around the empty islands.

Unique in Michigan geology, the ledges' mineral and fossil content have been studied by college students and rock hounds for generations.

Studied for footholds too. The hills of mid-Michigan are short on cliffs, so the ledges have been eagerly sought by climbers taking lessons or keeping in shape. They try out rappeling safety systems, belay principles, and knots, or anything else needed for an on-edge vertical life. Environmental and climbing ethics are part of it.

I'll walk, thanks. Up to forty to fifty feet high, the walls had a forbidding, old-castle look in the fading light of that particular visit, but are lovely on a clear morning, early spring, or after the curtain of leaves has fallen.

A photogenic railroad trestle provides train addicts (I'm one) an added tremble when a long freight thunders overhead. It happens often.

One-and-one-half miles from its starting point, the trail ends in town at the foot of Harrison Street, site of perennial gardens and a block from the Bridge Street bridge. On another day I found that the river has more parks and walking paths, Oak Park being the place to watch climbers.

Island Park, which held that Victorian Club Med of the early 1900s and drew trainloads of tourists, still gets lively many times a summer. Festivals are staged on the grounds, and a riverboat, the *Princess Laura* (one of a trio of riverboats plying the Greater Lansing area), docks here. *Laura* is a distinctly southern-style belle, carrying 112 passengers while banjos strum, the paddle wheel churns, and celebrations are going on.

Tourism, farming, and a certain amount of spillover from Lansing (only twelve miles to the state capitol building) are the core elements in Grand Ledge's past growth and present economy. Bridge Street carries the main business traffic, and directions are often given to shops or eateries as being "north of the river" or "south of the river." Antique shopping rates good to terrific, starting at the Church Street Antique Mall, north of the river. A non-profit cooperative in a renovated fire hall puts sixteen mini-shops together, giving an outlet for 125 local artists and crafty persons who paint, stuff their own dolls, make pottery, leaded glass, needlework, etc. Ledge Craft Lane, Inc., is on the corner of Bridge and River streets; 517-627-9843.

"Opera House" is often an upgrading term applied to any building where a show could be put on. The building on the east

Take a walking tour of historic homes

side of Bridge Street at River, however, did duty with melodramas, musicals, and graduations—even after starting off as a roller-skating rink. Today it houses the chamber of commerce, visitors center, reception hall, and Michigan Theater Barton Organ. A place for questions; telephone 517-627-2452.

Grand Ledge's modest downtown area had a major fire in 1993, leaving a wide gap facing Bridge Street. Happily, the façade of an old-timer bank remained sturdy enough to be allowed to stand, and present plans are to incorporate it into the replacement structure. That would be a neat touch.

A walking tour leaflet put out by the Grand Ledge Historical Society lists twenty-eight buildings, nearly all houses, which make for a sizable district in the National Register of Historic Places. Fifteen of these treasures are on Jefferson Street, including the public library and U. S. Post Office. There's a mural of more than passing interest in the post office, painted by Detroiter James Calder in 1939 depicting an earlier Grand Ledge. Trinity Episcopal Church, also on the list, has twelve Belgian glass windows with scenes from the life of Christ. To those who revere light filtered through jewel colors, these are real artworks.

Italianate, Queen Anne, Gothic, and Greek; Grand Ledge's tall trees and settled-in-solid look make the streets a treat for strollers. At 118 West Lincoln, a Greek Revival cottage built in 1880 houses the collection of the Grand Ledge Area Historical Society, the group that restored the building. It's open from 2:00 P.M. to 4:00 P.M. on Sundays or by special appointment; 517-627-5170 or 627-2452.

I went into Pasquale's on Bridge Street for a hearty Italian dinner and a chance to read over a list of Grand Ledge events. In June, the world's largest archery center gets busy. Apparently every archery expert this side of William Tell shows up to give their how-tos; 517-627-3251. Yankee Doodle Days fill up the last weekend in June. Our man Mudge gets his tribute with the "Mudge's Follies" musical production; add in antique cars, parade, carnival, craft show, general hoopla; 517-627-2579 or 627-2383. Twice a summer the Oneida Field Market spreads out informally with 200 exhibitors and free admission during the last weekends in June and September. The Island Art Fair on the first Saturday in August rounds up 135 crafters, music and riverboat rides.

Indian Summer Days last for the second weekend in October on Second Island, ringing with pioneer spirit, cider pressing, blacksmithing, and horse and buggy rides. And at Christmas, the Holiday Home Tour of six houses, antiques, and a bazaar takes place.

As a Lansing satellite, you know big motels are not far, but a charming bed and breakfast should be mentioned: Edward's Wind Crest, a farmhouse that grew and grew but remained a farm on the edge of town. Victorian gingerbread, turned posts, and comforts with country views from every window make this hostelry delightfully unique. It is located west of town at 11880 Oneida Road; 517-627-2666.

Go to the movies, rent a canoe, shop the farmers' market stands. There's always a country auction or garage sale somewhere nearby. Grand Ledge doesn't miss the roller coaster one bit.

Grand Ledge Chamber of Commerce (Greater Lansing):
517-627-2452

10

Holly: Goes Brightly

About an hour from downtown Detroit, minutes from Flint, halfway between I-75 and the US 23 freeways, the citizens of Holly are dangerously close to life's fast lane. Tucked behind square miles of green countryside, however, they prefer to smell the roses.

Holly *was* the fast lane in the 1800s, complete with big money, national recognition, and a few lucrative vices—hard to imagine if you arrive on a quiet June day when daisies bloom near the boarded-up depot and front porches have fresh coats of paint. On South Saginaw Street, the main north-south axis through town, a vintage fire station now houses civic offices and a visitors center. Along the block are the century-old red brick façades of offices and stores, still doing business with a newer set of tenants. Buggies tied up in the parking spaces would seem just right.

Three historic districts in Holly (they're working on a fourth) and nearly forty buildings are on the preservation list. Rather a large count for a village of 5,600.

In 1831 the Holly landscape was a gently rolling forest wilderness with dozens of small lakes. William and Sarah Gage were first to see its possibilities and bring their covered wagon to a halt. Six years later enough settlers had arrived to form a township, which civic leader Jonathon Allen christened "Holly" after his home in Mount Holly, New Jersey.

When a dam was built on the Shiawassie River providing waterpower for a sawmill, the township's prospects grew bright enough to lure other forms of enterprise plus a railroad Holly-deep into Michigan. The whole population came down to cheer the Detroit, Grand Haven, and Milwaukee's spiffy 1855 engine as it puffed into sight, pleased that such speedy (ten miles per hour) technology linked Holly with the world.

Other rail lines came around, taking out payloads of lumber and grain, chugging in with passengers, prestige, and prosperity.

The Père Marquette Railroad gave Holly an important boost when the company bought a locomotive in New York then shipped it west via the Erie Canal and plank roads just to have the engine's maiden trip made on their new tracks into Holly.

The first steel-rolled tracks ever laid in this country were used on the Holly-Flint line. Michigan Governor Crapo, a rail tycoon, showed faith by building an immense lumberyard. (The park on Broad Street is named for him.) Seventeen hotels with varying standards of comfort and decorum sprang up near the depot to compete for business from traveling gentry, salesmen, or opportunists with decks of cards. Passengers came to know Holly as the place where they changed trains or got into trouble.

Notes from the town history book tell of a devastating fire in 1875. The first "telephone" was that great old kids' gadget, two tomato cans and a cord strung between a bank and a hotel. Holly became an assembly center and the largest bicycle distributor in the United States. The Wixom Circus, Cole's World Shows, and the Robbins Circus picked Holly for their winter quarters. Bailey (Barnum's pal) built a mansion here.

Holly's summer charms brought families to area cottages when a big treat was the two-mile steamboat ride between Simonson and Bush lakes. (The connecting canal has vanished.)

On the darker side, eighteen saloons flourished mightily; so did gambling and the shady lady trade. Special trains ran out from

Detroit in the 1890s just for those eager to bet on illegal cockfights by lantern light while the law did a long blink. Barroom and street brawls were so common on one stretch of elbow-to-elbow saloons that the passage was nicknamed "Battle Alley," a name that stuck.

A major 1908 brouhaha involving a boisterous mob of circus roustabouts and gandy dancers was one mêlée too many. Alarmed citizens sent out a call to Kansas City's temperance crusader Carry Nation.

This time the feisty Mrs. Nation used an umbrella instead of an axe to smash bottles off shelves and let the demons of booze soak into the floor. She also stood on the corner berating (face-to-face) Governor Fred Warner on his laxness regarding liquor. It wasn't an overnight victory for the drys, but Holly moved into a more sober era. Today Carry is remembered with her own (not completely teetotaling) festival.

Grinnell Pianos, Cyclone Fences, White Star refinery, Hog Tractor, Detroit Battery—Holly had its share of big-name industries even as it was shrinking into retirement. Eventually they all faded away. Passenger trains quit coming, the station was boarded up, old saloons were turned into antique shops, most of the hotels vanished.

With one notable rescue: The Holly Hotel on Battle Alley was a burnt-out hulk when Linda Duman and George Kutlenlos bought the building in 1978 for restoration. Runaway optimism and hard work were clear winners. The Holly (a hotel in name only) is a Victorian prize, among the best restaurants in southern Michigan. Stained glass, red plush chairs, and rose carpeting fill the lounge, i.e. the "Dispensing Department," where a winsomely quaint though bare-breasted maiden's portrait hangs over the bar.

One dining corner seats patrons on old train seats beneath overhead luggage racks, but the main dining area is as genteel as a fur muff with ribbons.

President Bush ate here. So did baseball's Charlie Gehringer. I hope they started with the shrimp-stuffed mushrooms and went on to beef Wellington or poached Norwegian salmon. For reservations call 810-634-5208.

Lovely Holly

59

Next door the Battle Alley Arcade houses twenty-five antique dealers in cubbyhole shops along a "hallway" of old building fronts, an approach also used in Balcony Row Antiques on Broad Street where there are sixty more dealers at Water Tower Mall.

Other former saloon sites sell kitchen gadgets, clothing, Hawaiian shirts, Hong Kong specials. Note the U.S. bicentennial logo in the middle of the street and historic plaque nearby.

A brochure describing the history and contents of the Hadley House Museum and maps for a Holly walking tour are available on the second floor of the firehouse–visitors center. This is an interesting building. Look up into the tower where fire hoses once hung to dry. Downstairs the police used to keep prisoners in basement cells until a hopeful escapee became stuck in a furnace duct.

The walking tour takes you into the side streets to gaze at Italianate, Greek Revival, and Queen Anne homes of other decades, then past the little depot marking the first railroad junction in the state. There is said to have been a black marble fireplace in the ladies' waiting room. Men had a lunch counter on their side.

For railroading on another scale, meet the devotees bending over layouts, switches, and trestles in a Lilliputian world on Saginaw Street. Members of the Detroit Model Railroad Club open their doors on special days to train buffs. Ask for more details at the visitors center.

Holly puts all this nostalgia to profitable use with the Carry Nation Festival, the promotion of a nearby Renaissance Fest (fair damsels, jousting knights, medieval goodies), and a Dickens Olde Fashioned Christmas Festival that would melt Scrooge. Storytellers, a fantasy parade, sleigh rides, actual Victorian weddings, etc., carry the spirit through four weekends between Thanksgiving and Christmas.

At the four-day party in Carry's name, her sobriety visit is reenacted in a thirty-minute pageant while sassy cancan dancers wink at old straight-laced inhibitions.

Add to the festivities a Blues Fest in June, an annual Holly Canoe Race, and the Arts and Crafts Fair in November. The Blues gala's slogan "blues, booze, and bar-b-ques" probably makes Carry's ghost want to rattle an extra chain.

Thousands of visitors come through for these doings, labeling the village "City of Festivals."

The town is not a total museum for nineteenth-century Americana. Drive-in food, shopping plazas, etc., fill a variety of needs ranging from tastes for Big Macs to a wide selection of computer equipment in nonhistoric (the north end) parts of town.

Holly residents should be in prime health with golden tans by July; they are within hiking or biking distance of four dozen lakes (five within village limits), state recreation areas, and hills high enough to turn this into a major ski center for southeastern Michiganians. They are also close to summer beaches, fresh farm produce, orchards, woods, trails, golf, cider mills, and wineries.

Holly Area Chamber of Commerce: 810-634-1900
Michigan Renaissance Festival: 810-645-9640
State Park Recreation Area Information: 517-373-1220

11

L'Anse: A Gate With Two Options

Nearing the end of its long run from Miami, Florida, US 41 cuts through the thick and murmuring Ottawa National Forest, past the path to Canyon Falls, past the Michigan Technological University's Forestry Center. The road rises and dips through its long green slot, then curves rather suddenly toward wide blue Keweenaw Bay, one of the major inlets of the Great Lakes.

It is this moody arm of Lake Superior that makes a peninsula of the land west of it and sets the legendary Copper Country as a place apart.

Assigned a niche between cliffs and hills at the foot of Keweenaw Bay, the town of L'Anse (pronounced *Lahnse*) does eastern sentry duty for upper northwest Michigan. Beyond its west side lies the Keweenaw Peninsula, Porcupine Mountains, ski hills, and towns at ease with semiwilderness.

Directly northward are the east-side bay regions. Passing through L'Anse is the only way to reach the tiny hamlets in the Huron Mountains, up where there are no US highways and where Arvon and Curwood mountains are Michigan's highest points; God's country, hinterlands, moose territory, and all that.

The entrance to town angles off to the right at US 41 and Broad Street, where L'Anse's Visitors Information Center doubles as the Baraga County Museum. Take a glance-around course in area history and geology before helping yourself to lists of fishing spots (fourteen kinds of fish and fifty-five places to catch them on one brochure), bed and breakfast folders, or sight-seeing suggestions.

Several shady blocks downhill from there, Main Street sports the only light in town—a blinker four-way stop. Drugstore, hardware store, etc., are of substantial size; you know you can do business in this place. One block straight ahead on the waterfront a small park is large enough for a bandshell. Singing groups, combos, and soloists take over the stage on Thursday evenings every summer, their bright sounds echoing far up the bay.

Turn right at the blinker. Near the high-school playing field the Baraga County courthouse sits as though it were on a shelf just uphill on another street. The well-tended homes of longtime citizens line the way out of town.

Of the 4,000 souls in L'Anse township, 450 are Native American, united in strong tribal ties. Across the bay in Baraga, Native Americans run a popular gambling casino, an eighty-room motel, and a trading post, plus their own affairs on reservation lands. They are one of the county's major employers.

The biggest manufacturer in town is Celotex-Fiberboard, a far cry from the historic fur business that got L'Anse under way. This was a trading post for trappers in the early 1800s, one of those small wedges that cracked the shell of the north for Europeans.

The widespread North West Company built a post in 1800 that lasted until after the War of 1812. Thirty years later the American Fur Trading Company decided they too needed to set up shop at the south end of Keweenaw Bay, and sent Quebec-born Peter Crebassa, who brought his bride, Nancy. Madame Crebassa was clearly made of extraordinary stuff, traveling by canoe through bad weather, black flies, and treacherous rocks to live among unknown people at the edge of the forest.

The missionary-minded Peter read his Bible to a local chief who came to hear it, explaining the words as best he could, while sending persistent messages to Father Baraga, the closest priest,

180 miles away in Wisconsin: "Come and help!" Baraga came in 1843, then returned soon after to establish a mission and build a log church and a school.

The fur trade dimmed, other industries (lumbering, fishing) grew. By the mid-1800s L'Anse was on its way. Meanwhile, the priest became the Bishop Baraga, revered for his willingness to don snowshoes and trudge icy miles to his duties. The county and a town chose to name themselves "Baraga," and more than 130 years later in 1972 a shrine was erected near L'Anse in his honor.

This was not without difficulty, however. As a thirty-five-foot hand-wrought bronze statue of Baraga was being hoisted into place atop a set of rainbowlike laminated beams (rising from five concrete wigwams) the hem of the Father's cassock caught on the base. A torch was lit to free the statue, but insulation inside the figure caught fire. Warmer than he ever was in real life, the bishop's near-cremation was averted (considered a miracle by some) and his heroic visage now looks out over the bay from atop a cliff on the south side of US 41. A small coffee shop selling locally crafted gifts and books about the bishop stands nearby.

On the walls of the town hall on Main Street hang scenes of early L'Anse. For anyone locked into earnest research, the school library and Baraga County Public Library are one and the same, housing a substantial 14,000 volumes.

L'Anse is so close to the community life north of it, a drive to visit the high spots is almost like a tour through the suburbs.

Up Pequaming Road about nine miles on a small sub-peninsula, Henry Ford tried putting part of a pet scheme to work; he thought his company should own the source of all raw materials that went into Ford cars. Rubber plantations for tires, iron mines for the steel, etc. Here in Michigan was wood for station-wagon paneling and other uses, and Pequaming had a ready-made waterside village with a sawmill. Ford bought the whole community layout plus 400,000 wooded acres, then ran his company town as though it were a strict school. It was seen to that everything appeared spotless and proper when Mr. Ford paid a visit.

Which he did. The Bungalow, a roomy cottage overlooking

The statue of Bishop Baraga in L'Anse

Keweenaw Bay was one of his retreats, sometimes in the company of pals Harvey Firestone and Thomas Edison.

Ford's plan for an independent manufacturing empire didn't make it (the collapse of that vision is the subject for another book), and the model town is long gone, replaced by private dwellings. The Bungalow lucked out. The twenty-room house lives again as a bed and breakfast big enough for seminar gatherings. Sit on the porch and talk with the big-wheel ghosts after contacting owner Lora Hartman for details; 906-524-7595.

One detail *I* can give in advance: the fishing and hiking are fabulous.

Backtracking southward slightly, turn east on Skanee Road. A short detour to the Indian Cemetery may be of interest, but be sure to step softly, as though you were wearing moccasins, and respect the low mounds. For a long time the Indians buried their dead on the hills overlooking Lake Superior, but as the Europeans arrived, those whose home this was began to carry them inland.

It was supposed to take the buried loved one five days to reach the happy hunting ground, so at one time small pine houses were erected over graves to provide shelter for their journey. That practice has disappeared, but a few houses may be seen at Brimley (eastern Upper Peninsula).

On Huron Bay, a much narrower inlet than Keweenaw Bay, the hamlet of Skanee (named for the Swedish province of Skone) never quite made it into the mainstream. Not even slightly. Early comers paddled here in canoes, later on boats, or they hiked Indian trails along the shoreline hoping to land jobs in timber, commercial fishing, or working the substantial slate deposits nearby.

Some hankered for a little farmland, having been told how great conditions were for growing things—which wasn't quite so. There was an assumption—held especially dear by the timber barons who owned the land—that after "axe, saw, and fire the cloverlands" would prosper. Some apple orchards and potato farms actually did make money for a while, but farming is not very notice-able along these roads.

What should be noticed here are the Skanee Town Hall, now

on the National Register of Historic Sites (the town hall's collection of old farm and lumber scenes are worth more than a dozen textbooks), the restored Skanee School, and Zion Lutheran Church, oldest of the American Synod in Michigan. When the Scandinavians and Finns arrived, new churches were decidedly Lutheran, each with services at least partly in the founding group's language. There is little evidence that those Swedes and Finns had any ecumenical leanings. It might even be that rivalry relieved the boredom of long winters.

You can get to the top of Curwood and Arvon mountains but you won't see much because the hills are heavily forested. An old bumpy logging trail suffices as a road up Mount Curwood; proceed at your own risk. The mountain is privately owned and permission should be secured before you start off. Mount Arvon's north-side trail goes up to 1,978 feet, the "peak" of the state. Unless someone has improved signs as of this writing, the trail is an easy way to get good and lost.

There is plenty of hiking and camping in these hills and shores, and when rain dampens your zeal, go bowling at the Ojibwa's Whirl-I-Gig Lanes on the road of the same name in Skanee.

Take time for a pasty (rhymes with *nasty*) or plate of fresh brook trout. Cookin' hearty is a way of life, testified to by the pie-size sweet rolls served at the Hilltop Restaurant on US 41 (attached to a motel; call 800-424-2548). Or sit down in Kathy's Village Restaurant (524-5455) or Tony's Steakhouse (524-9900) and harken to those "Yuper" accents. Upper Peninsula natives give their own lilt to the language. Don't worry too much about calling ahead; in L'Anse dining reservations are needed every fourth leap year.

The other way to go from L'Anse, westward around the bay into Copper Country, can be enchanting on a warm sunny day or in the fall. (See Chapter 2 for more information on Copper Country.) If you are still looking for a place to eat I recommend the dining room of the Baraga Lakeside Inn.

Over twenty waterfalls can be found in Baraga County, some with very easy trails to them, such as the path to Canyon Falls back south a few miles on US 41. Another joy to hikers is Sturgeon Gorge, the deepest cut in Michigan and deeply hidden by the forest. Take US 41 to Baraga Plains cut-off road, go left at Four Corners, then follow the signs to the start of a trail.

Two more spots before leaving L'Anse's county: drive fifteen miles north of Baraga on US 41, then six or seven miles west on Amheim road (be patient), then south as the sign indicates. For this you get to visit a genuine old Finnish farmstead, original, restored, and remarkable. On the National Register of Historic Sites, it looks the way it did in 1920, which was not much different than the way it looked in 1899.

The Hanka farm represents the tough life and hard work of Mina and Herman and their family. Herman worked (and was injured) in copper mining to earn money to buy these eighty acres where the sauna was probably completed before the house. Including a log smokehouse, blacksmith shop, milk house, etc., the little compound is open for tours from Memorial Day through mid-October. Please bring a dollar.

Baraga County Tourist and Recreation Association, 755 East Broad Street, L'Anse, MI 49946; 906-524-7444

12

Leland: Trying to Stay Small

The east side of Michigan has the "thumb"; the west side has a "little finger." It's the Leelanau Peninsula, a gift of earth pushed up between the fingers of a glacier in an age when ice was shaping the Great Lakes.

And how extremely sweet it is!

A county off by itself, hilly Leelanau's charms are wrapped in flowering fruit trees every spring, gleam with golden hardwoods every fall. Named by pioneer Henry Schoolcraft's Chippewa wife, Leelanau's ("light of life") scenery is a carefully tended collage of vineyards and wineries, rolling acres of apple and cherry orchards (the dark tart beauties that come mostly from Michigan), and 100 miles of hypnotic coast. Photogenic waterside stretches encompass the Sleeping Bear Dunes, towering regions of sand that have become a National Lakeshore treasure, and the Manitou Islands in Lake Michigan.

There are beaches with Petoskey stones (the official state rock), pristine inland lakes, historic villages, and (these days especially) an air of poignancy. In an era of dream hideaways, Leelanau's old-timers are feeling the pinch of development and wondering how to embrace progress while holding on to the factors so basic to their appeal.

Leelanau and Leland, the county seat, are almost too good

to be true; that's not a comfortable idea. Leland, once spelled "Leeland" because of its sheltered position near the shore of Lake Michigan, can be hiked around in sixty minutes. Plainly, no one should take less than an afternoon, because there is so much to poke through, so many spots to sit and enjoy.

Ships were sailing past Leland's townsite in the early 1800s, not always making it past the shoals of the Manitous during heavy weather. The U.S. government built a lighthouse on nearby South Manitou Island in 1839. Around this time Antoine Manseau and John Miller decided to build a dam on the Carp River (now the Leland River) to harness power for their lumber mill. The stream connected Lake Leelanau to the big lake, so their private barricade blocked off any future boat traffic. By the mid-1870s an estimated 5,000 loggers were working these woods. Loggers are long gone but the dam still lives on.

Other folks with other interests came at a slightly slower pace. A missionary priest built Holy Trinity Church for the Indians in 1870. When the Leland Lake Superior Iron Company started operating in the area and a rail connection was made with Traverse City, the little community was really under way. Commercial fishing and the attention of "summer people" from the midwestern middle-to-upper crust brought income plus considerable prestige.

These families, escaping summers in Chicago or St. Louis, had money, servants, education, and time; they built a substantial and solid society. A short walk around Leland and the close-by village of Lake Leelanau and you know you're in Norman Rockwell's kind of setting. Not-always-fast food; no discount stores til the end of summer when there are some sharp markdowns in the boutiques.

The settled-in ambience, careful preservation, and nostalgia of Leland draws several thousand visitors a year. The town has managed to keep things spiffy and clean without going all-out touristy. Below the dam, where the river empties into Lake Michigan, an area called "Fishtown" is a case in point.

There are still traces of true commercial fishing boats tied up among the fancy pleasure craft, a gray wooden dockside, etc., even though most of the former fishing shanties (with their falling shingles re-attached) have been turned into little shops. Real nets are strung around big squarish spindles to dry, and you can purchase fresh salmon or lake trout at Carlson Fisheries, but behind those weathered walls it's mostly T-shirts with slogans and yogurt fantasies. True shantytown life is as gone as the carrier pigeon, a bird once found in these areas by the hundreds of thousands.

Today the Fisherman's Cove Restaurant hugs the harbor and dam, the sounds of the waterfall serving as pleasant background music. Call 616-256-9866. A Michigan match for any old New England small hotel, the Riverside Inn (615-256-9971) and Bluebird Restaurant (616-256-9081) with their porches overlooking the river are other waterside spots with flavor-driven cooks. Both know exactly how to treat a whitefish.

Fishtown shops edge along a parking lot, a large sheltered boat-basin, children's playground, and picnic tables. Here's where you make reservations and pick up tickets to South Manitou. Plan ahead; the extremely popular (in July and August, it's a top state attraction) Manitou Transit's ferry, the *Miche-Mokwa*, has a limited schedule—chancy for anyone who waits til the last minute before deciding to go. Call 616-256-9116.

According to Indian lore, a fierce fire on the west shore of Lake Michigan forced a mother bear with two cubs to swim across. The youngsters struggled but just couldn't make it. When Mamma Bear, keeping vigil on the shore, finally fell asleep, the Great Spirit (Manitou) turned her into a giant sand dune, while the drowning cubs became islands, never far from their mother.

A special spirit certainly visits here. Sixteen miles offshore from Leland, there are few retreats to match the Manitous, part of the National Lakeshore Park system. The islands add up to about 20,000 acres of reclaimed wilderness; vest-pocket samplings of the way it was. Only faint traces of former farms and logging interests poke their clues up from fields or inlet. Cries of herring gulls and soft surf may be all you'll hear through tall cedar, maple, and elder woodlands. Along the shore of south Manitou the hull of the *Frisco Morizon* is still visible. Scores of other shipwreck remnants fill the surrounding waters. Birds, rare plants, a splendid lighthouse; there is enough here (or not here) to satisfy nature buffs, history addicts, or any seeker of solitude.

Great Lakes' sailors in Leland Harbor

Leland: Trying to Stay Small

No regular ferry runs as of this writing, but charter boats can take you over to North Manitou where harbor improvements have been recently made.

Back on the mainland, shopping conforms to slightly pricey expectations. Tasteful and very often handcrafted items include beautiful jewelry and leather, pottery, and extra touches for your boat's cabin. The Mainstreet Gallery at the south end of town is walled in the work of regional artists. At Leland's center, the Tin Soldier stands guard over upscale gifts; the Last Straw dips into batik watercolors, original and traditional wheat-weaving, jewels, and ceramics. Browse through Inland Passage, and Pratt's. I'm partial to the wares of Leelanau Books myself.

The Leelanau Historical Museum at 203 East Cedar Street retraces local history in light, bright displays. The intricate and beautiful craftwork of native tribes draws more respect every time you see it. Call 616-256-9895.

Nobody with an extra day comes without a jaunt to the end of the peninsula and the Grand Traverse Lighthouse Museum. This is the best beach for finding Petoskey stones, which aren't really stones but clusters of old coral. Unlike other coral, these will buff up and can be chiseled. If you suspect you've found one, just wet its surface and you can be sure.

As you wind back to Leland, peninsula wineries urge you to stop in for a taste test. Leelanau Limited, the largest in northwest Michigan, and L. Mawby's are west of Suttons Bay. The Good Harbor Vineyards and Boskydel (open all year) both have Lake Leelanau addresses.

Another dining choice could be the Leland Lodge, a comfortable dining room overlooking the Leland Country Club, where the public is welcome to play golf.

Though there are more places to stay within a short drive from Leland than there are cherries in a twenty-inch pie, several very good bed and breakfast places in the area shouldn't go unmentioned. The Highlands, on North Lake Street, sits in a grove of tall white pines overlooking Lake Michigan, six blocks north of the Cove Restaurant. Not many rooms, so try early; telephone

616-256-7632 or 313-292-5503. The Snowbird Inn, two miles south of town on State 22, serves gourmet breakfasts and will pack you a box lunch for your day. Rooms are limited; call 616-256-9462. The big multifaceted Homestead (with five restaurants) on the Lake Michigan shore is just down the road and still within the county. Or try Sugar Loaf Ski and Summer Resort.

A calendar of events in Leland is almost beside the point. There are celebrations on the Fourth of July, boat races and art-in-the-park shows, musical moments. I get the feeling, however, that if a person needs a special parade to spruce up enjoyment of Leland and Leelanau County there's something not quite alive in their heads.

Leelanau County Chamber of Commerce: 616-256-9895
Traverse City Convention & Visitors Bureau (includes all adjoining counties): 800-TRAVERS or 616-947-1120

13

Ludington:
Ferry Tale Town

A favorite scene of the Michigan summer drama is played out daily in Ludington, sitting placidly halfway up the west Michigan coast. By 6:30 A.M. skies have turned up to full daylight (well, there *are* cloudy days now and then), sailboats and fishing charters are pulling out of the Ludington Lake channel into Lake Michigan, cars have already lined up to be driven aboard a great black-hulled ferry for a four-hour ride to Manitowoc, Wisconsin.

By 7:25 A.M. as many as 500 passengers have trotted up the iron steps to the main deck (or used the handicap elevator), a thick plume of black smoke pours from the stack as a historic vessel using a vintage engine, and the whistle—in the best cruise ship manner—gives a booming blast.

At 7:30 A.M. the 410-foot *Badger* ventures into an unsalted sea to spend a couple of hours beyond sight of any land; a first-person chance to see how great a Great Lake really is, the nearest thing to an ocean voyage most midwest Americans will ever experience. Those not at the rails to watch the landmarks of Ludington fade away are lined up in the Upper Deck Café for a buffet breakfast, buzz in and out of the ship's museum and souvenir shop, or settle into card games. Others find a deck chair, tuck themselves under stadium blankets, and snooze. A movie or video room and video-game room amuses those on withdrawal from real experience.

If this seems to be a lot of detail regarding a Ludington attraction while ignoring the town, it's not. "Boats R Ludington," especially big ferries that have been steaming out of its harbor over one hundred years. Ask around. There isn't a citizen of long standing that hasn't had a brother, uncle, grandfather, son, or husband working on one of the ships. The biggest employers in town are the Mason County Hospital and Dow Chemical, but working on the boats or surviving an infamous storm ties together the heritages.

The first European craft to pull up to Ludington's wide sand shore was the birch bark canoe of priest-explorer Père Jacques Marquette. With fellow-priest Jolliet, Marquette had gone along the west bank of Lake Michigan to the now-Chicago area, and followed leads to the Mississippi River, breaking open the secrets of a new land. Forced back by illness, the dying Marquette made a final landing near an Ottawa Indian village, a site now marked by a forty-five-foot white cross. His body was later returned to St. Ignace for reburial.

One hundred fifty years later another European, Aaron Burr Caswell, arrived by schooner. He wasn't alone for long. The tempting opportunities of pine-covered land plus a good harbor brought other lumbermen just as soon as Caswell lifted his axe. One ambitious fellow, James Ludington, set up a sawmill on the edge of the forest, planned the town, and put his name on everything. Because of its convenient position on the coast and ready supplies of food and fuel, Ludington enjoyed boom years as a port and as the seat of Mason County.

In 1875 the Flint & Père Marquette Railroad started putting its boxcars on ferries from Ludington to Sheboygan, Wisconsin, an idea that spread to other railroads and cities on the lake. Sixteen routes and ports became interlocked with freight and ferry service.

Sixty-five years after train ferries started, the world's largest car ferry of its time, the *City of Midland*, was launched into service at Ludington. The *City of Midland* was perfect for vacationers, with a deck for cars, passenger accommodations, small staterooms, and dining. After World War II, two more ships were built:

the 410-foot SS *Spartan* and SS *Badger*, at a cost of $5 million apiece. In peak times the fleet (going all year) made 7,000 lake crossings, toting thousands of passengers and autos along with 200,000 freight cars.

Although train ferries avoided delays in getting freight around Chicago, their day was dying. Expensive vessel upkeep, advances in rail technology, truckers and motorists on a competitive interstate highway system were reasons cited by the Chesapeake and Ohio Railroad (but not by Ludington ferry owners) for starting abandonment procedures. When they finally quit, two new owners bravely kept things going until they went bankrupt, and the three ships were confiscated to pay bills.

It looked like the end of a hundred-year era until financier Charles Conrad, of Grand Rapids, stepped in, wrestling the matter through the courts. Conrad worked on the boats as a young man. He knew the rapport and outright love that went into running them. Conrad won the right to refurbish the *Badger* and in May 1992, resumed service, sans rail freight.

Morale in Ludington went into overdrive. Their ferry meant tourist dollars, but beyond that, community affection for the big boat was genuine. Today the town is the center of a flotilla; fifty-five charter boats based in Ludington Harbor, hundreds of pleasure boats (sails, outboards, canoes) nearby.

A *long* pier with a lighthouse at the end lets you walk far out to see the sand dunes up and down the coast, watch boaters, fish, or gaze at sunsets.

A Historic White Pine Village on a bluff overlooking Lake Michigan south of town and other aspects of Ludington life come forward. The collection of twenty historic buildings has a few replicas in the mix, but you can't tell pretend from the genuine on the short paths between them: a one-room school (real), an 1880 farmhouse (real), a trapper's cabin (real), the Phoenix Hose Company (firehouse replica). Everything inside is for sure ye olde, be they tools or postal furnishings.

Unusual gem for any historic village is the first Mason County Courthouse standing on its original land. The two-story structure

Take the Ludington ferry across Lake Michigan to Wisconsin

was built in 1849 by A. B. Caswell, mentioned above, and is now a national historic site.

White Pine festivals include a May salute to the car ferries, a Civil War Muster in July, and the great August get-together of the Scottsville Clown Band and Pentwater Civic Band, filling the air with music while the village staff serves buckets of ice cream. To get there take Iris Road off South Père Marquette Highway (old

US 31) to South Lakeshore Drive then north to the Village; telephone 616-843-4808.

A sister institution, the Rose Hawly Museum, in downtown Ludington, tries hard to fill in the Mason County historic gaps. Lumber camps and farms have their own research sections in the archives; the paraphernalia of their times documented and sealed into glass cases. Indians, settlers, seamen, and trainmen, the folklore and facts of a town wedged between woods and water are given tender care. The museum is found on Loomis Street between Rath and James; telephone 616-843-2001.

Walk around this solid, settled town awhile. The Mason County Courthouse was built in 1895 and is well worth a look inside. Elsewhere on tree-shaded Ludington Street there are lovely old houses speaking well of Ludington's past. The grandest of them all, a Greek Revival beauty with four pillars rising past a second-floor balcony, is on the market as of this writing, and I am hoping that someone with bed and breakfast ambitions snatches it up.

Between the third week in June and Labor Day, a bright red double-decker English bus waits at the corner of James and Ludington, ready to take riders south to Pentwater or north a short piece to the Ludington State Park, one of the treasures of Michigan's park system; telephone 616-845-1231 for full schedule and details.

Keep walking toward the lake, pausing for homage to a superb product at the House of Flavors: ice cream from your dreams; addiction at one lick. It's also a good place for breakfast, lunch, or whatever.

On the north edge of town, Ludington State Park sparkles with six miles of Lake Michigan beach, four miles of shore on Hamlin Lake. Hike the scenic trail to the highly photogenic black and white Point Sable Lighthouse. Jog, rent a canoe, sunbathe, visit the nature center for movies and gift items. A fine lookout point requires some stair climbing but the end result is worth every huff and puff.

True believers head for the expansive Nordhouse Dunes (cars aren't allowed) to follow ten miles of trails through the wildflowers and fauna of a special environment. For park information call 616-843-8671.

On the east side of Ludington are all the fast-food and discount stores needed to sustain life. Slower but better is Gibbs for real food cooked by Grandma (maybe) and down home hospitality. Open seven days a week, Gibbs offers to pick you up if you're boating or flying into town. Call 616-845-0311.

Since the ferry leaves almost at daybreak, staying at a Ludington Motel is practically mandatory. Among the recommended are the Viking Arms motel on East Ludington, 616-843-3441; Miller's Lakeside Motel, across from the pier, 616-843-3458; Ventura Motel, 616-845-5124, or 800-968-1440; Synder's Shoreline Inn, 616-845-1261; Parkview Cottages by the Lake, 616-843-4445. Summer is the top of the season so expect things to be a little pricey.

Driving away from Ludington has pleasant country options. Going south on US 31, detour west on Iris Road to Lakeshore, then walk up the hill at the hydroelectric facility's lookout point, 370 feet above Lake Michigan. Picnic tables and camping are nearby. Or zig-zag through the back roads as you go west or north to find fresh-picked fruit, and U-pick opportunities on inviting lanes through a rumpled quilt of green hills; that is, after you've waved goodbye to the SS *Badger* and promised to come back.

SS *Badger* passenger reservations and information: 800-841-4243
or 616-845-5555
Ludington Area Chamber of Commerce: 800-542-4600 or
616-845-0324

14

Mackinac Island City:
One Season for Itself

Beer . . . fuel . . . milk . . . soup . . . I squinted through a freezing mask of air and braced my feet on the ice-coated upper deck of a ferry to Mackinac Island, watching men trundle carts of supplies from a St. Ignace parking lot onto the cargo level.

"Looks like you're expecting a blizzard to cut you off from the world," I called.

"Could happen!" was the answer.

Mackinac Island, one of the last resort spots of its kind in North America, is already cut off from the world, even in mid-summer; cut off from automobiles, billboards, fast food, six-choice cinema theaters, and two-thirds of the twentieth century.

For 150 years vacationers have come by the thousands to this forested jewel island up where Lake Michigan and Lake Huron merge and Michigan's two peninsulas are close to touching; where time leans back to horse and buggies, Victorian houses, candy kitchens, and rocking chairs on wide front porches.

The town seen by summer visitors as the ferry pulls into harbor is not a movie set; it just looks like one with a whitewashed fort on a green hilltop, church steeple, and picket fences beyond a forest of sailboat masts. Nineteenth-century storefronts line the business blocks. Bikers and buggies fill the streets. There isn't a car in sight. Flowers edge the wide lawns.

Everything is as crisp and clean as a new bedsheet.

Eighty-six percent of the isle (eight miles around the edge) is a Michigan state park, a rock hill covered with pine and spruce, laced with paths and trails. A golf course and small airport are in the center.

Harbor and town are on the island's south side, with rims of private homes going up the east and west bluffs. Some of these "cottages" are Queen Anne mansions, the stuff of a preservationist's dream. Hotels large and small, bed and breakfasts, restaurants, and shops make Mackinac (say Macki*naw*) a lively colony from midspring to midfall, known far beyond our Michigan or even U.S. borders.

The town I saw on that cold day was far different. Snow covered the grass; hardly anything was moving. Houses had their shades drawn. I could see chairs piled on the tables in the Chippewa Hotel. No carriages, just parked snowmobiles.

The shouts of men putting supplies onto wagons and the stamping feet of the big Percherons who would pull the load broke through the quiet. (Carriage horses, about 550 of them, spend their winters on mainland farms.)

The scene was deceiving. Behind the doors of the town hall, in the school on the hill, in unseen kitchens, the real Mackinac Island City was going about its business, answering mail, doing laundry, rehearsing the Christmas program.

A lot of people think (and I was one of them) that when winter came everyone went home except maintenance men and a few hermit types. Not so. After a spring, summer, and fall filled with selling souvenirs, serving meals, conducting tours, and turning down beds, winter hospitality turns inward. A tight-knit community of about 600 humans takes a well-earned breather. This is when children and grandchildren of times past (plus a scattering of determined newcomers) draw the string tightly around their own kind and fish or hunt together, catch up on their bookkeeping, or play bingo down at the town hall.

Mackinac Island City: One Season for Itself

They started their hiatus with a rousing ceremony, bringing the pool table, which has been stored all summer to make room for lunch tables, back into the Mustang Lounge. Cheers and toasts all around. The grocery store, drugstore, and Mustang are the only downtown businesses to stay open all year. Four out of the twenty-three island hostelries are open for cross-country skiers.

In this special town (actually called the City of Mackinac Island) children and teens attend the kindergarten-to-twelfth grade school in an area called Harrisonville where most of the permanent homes are. Many are descendants of the Indians or early French settlers. There's a medical clinic (with a standard ambulance), ready to fix broken legs or give flu shots. Babies are born on the island but moms-to-be are encouraged to go to the mainland two weeks ahead of time for more complete facilities.

The city's civic structure is the same as anywhere else; chamber of commerce, mayor, and city council. The volunteer fire department uses an up-to-date fire engine, although crew members may have to bike their way to the station. In a settlement of wooden structures, they have an excellent track record.

I rather expected to see cars sneak out of hiding. None. The time warp only goes so far, however, and winter is for snowmobiles, which zip around as though their owners' autoless lives left a speed vacuum.

A Christmas bazaar is held in early December; at the center of town a brightly lit tree stands in a snowy intersection where closed stores and drawn shades give the scene an otherworldly look.

By January the ice between the island and St. Ignace is usually thick enough to hold hikers or even snowmobiles, following a five-mile path marked by family Christmas trees. (Don't try the trip alone or in murky weather.)

By March the ice bridge is gone; soon after that the first ferry crosses. The first spring travelers arrive.

Like doting oldsters who were glad to see the grandchildren leaving after the last holiday and are now happy to see them back, townspeople greet visitors with genuine warmth; they've had their long coffee break.

Winter: Mackinac Island City

However, Mackinac Island City is not just a town anymore. Its citizens are part of living history in a settlement like no other. Once the Native Americans held powwows and sacred rites on this island. It has been claimed by the French and the British (who built the fort), was a base for John Jacob Astor's lucrative fur business and the center of a lively fishing industry.

That faded when fishing for travelers became more lucrative. William Cullen Bryant declared ". . . the manifest destiny of Mackinac Island is to be a watering place. . . ." A soldier wrote in 1830, "It is so healthy here that a person has to get off the island to die."

Such word-of-mouth reviews had a strong effect. The Protestant mission building was converted to a hotel in 1852 and more followed. Wealthy passengers on new luxury steamboats loved the rugged north but demanded comforts; Mackinac Island gave it to them, becoming *the* place to summer.

When the Grand Hotel (built by a consortium of railroad financiers) opened, a few high-born ladies and their maids who couldn't get rooms even slept in the hallway rather than miss this supreme social event. The Grand, host to movie stars and moguls, the media's darling, gleaming in summer with yellow awning, red geraniums, and liveried footmen, has the world's longest front porch (116 feet). The movie *Somewhere in Time* hinted at life in the Grand although much of it was actually filmed at Mission Point Resort, another rather grand place to stay and hold meetings at the other side of town.

History, natural and human, unfolds as you explore the island back roads and museums: Arch Rock, "Sugarloaf," Fort Mackinac, Dr. William Beaumont's House, historic churches (St. Anne's Catholic, Trinity Episcopal, Mission Church, and the Bark Chapel). These are just some of the samplings from a long list.

Year-round residents are wonderful sources of local history if you don't bother them when they're flipping fudge or renting out rooms. Winter is best for remembering how it was or what their great grandfathers did here. (Their fathers were probably in tourism too.) Very few have ever wanted to live anywhere else.

For those of us who can only visit, a few tips: reserve well ahead of time, know what events are going on, bring a raincoat and warm jacket . . . just in case.

There are 1,000 rooms in Mackinac Island City. The Grand Hotel's regal price includes a lavish breakfast and dinner; no tips but an 18 percent surcharge is added to the bill. Telephone 906-847-3331. Mission Point Resort (see the lobby even if you can't check in) guests enjoy full breakfast buffets; telephone 906-847-3312.

At the Iroquois there are great views of the harbor and Mackinac Bridge. Telephone 906-847-3321. The Chippewa Hotel ("Chip"), next to the marina, is favored by boaters with its excellent dining and nighttime glow; call 906-847-3341. A registered historic site, the Island House charms everyone; 906-847-3347. The midtown Murray Hotel, decorated with romantic antiques, is close to all the action; 906-847-3361. The Windemere Hotel is about as close as you can come to staying in one of the old houses on the bluff. The inn's owner comes from an island "first" family; you are a guest in a very special home; 906-847-3301. There are many more, plus bed and breakfast houses.

For those braving winter winds there is the Voyageur Inn, 906-847-6175; Bogan Lane Inn (not guaranteed open), 906-847-3439; Pontiac Lodge, 906-847-3364; Stonecliffe, on Christmas and New Year's Day, 907-847-3355.

Rejoice that there will seldom be television in your room—not even at the Grand or Mission Point, although there are usually lounge rooms for those who need their fix. Telephones aren't standard either, but are more common.

Have a good inexpensive hamburger at the Mustang or Horn's Gaslight Bar. Hotel dining rooms are tops, almost without exception. For an unforgettable event, pay the $40 plus, dress up in your Gucci best, and strut between the mirrored pillars of "peacock alley" at the Grand Hotel. Sumptuous food, naturally. Personally, I am plotting to kidnap the chef at Mission Point.

Mull over this shortened calendar:

During June, the sweet-smelling Lilac Festival takes place as well as the Mackinac Island Chamber Music Festival which lasts two weeks. Over on the mainland the St. Ignace Antique Auto Show—*big* show—runs during the last weekend of the month.

During July there are fireworks on Independence Day, and

Mackinac Island City: One Season for Itself

two big boat races: the Chicago-to-Mackinac Yacht Race, the third weekend; Port Huron-to-Mackinac Race on the fourth weekend.

In August, there are bicycle races and a horse show, and a special ferry takes guests to the antique boat show in Hessel on the second weekend in the month.

The big local event in September is the Labor Day Bridge Walk when thousands of Michiganians hike between peninsulas on the Mackinac Bridge.

The island is a wonderful place for fall color, end-of-season sales in the shops, change of pace. By Halloween it's nearly over, and town folks are giving each other that are-you-holding-up? look.

November is the final winding down. The island turns to quiet. The community recaptures its essence. There's still time to go hunting. Repair things at home. Vote.

It's a town again.

For more information on bed and breakfasts, ferries, events, tours, the weather, horseback rides, summer jobs, or whatever: buy a copy of "Mackinac Connection: An Insider's Guide," by Amy McVeigh. She says it all.

Mackinac Island City Chamber of Commerce: 906-847-3787
St. Ignace Area Tourist Association: 906-643-8717
Mackinac Area Tourist Bureau: 616-436-5664 (note: Mackinaw
    City in the lower peninsula is the only one spelled with a w.
    There are hundreds of additional rooms in both these
    ferry-to-Mackinac Island cities)

15

Marshall:
Capital Ideas

There isn't another town like Marshall, Michigan, where one citizen built his house for the tropics, and another built a governor's mansion that never housed a governor. Few towns began with such rich and educated groundbreakers. Few towns have had to survive such drastic changes in their economic lives.

Few are as admired.

In 1830 Sidney Ketchum left a wealthy upstate New York family to travel along Michigan's North Territorial Road looking for a good place to create a business and a political center. Ketchum knew that Michigan would become a state soon and wanted to be in on the ground floor. He chose a verdant spot where Rice Creek merged with the Kalamazoo River, one with shipping possibilities and good mill sites. Then he convinced his brother George to come help chop down trees and keep the books. Together they plotted out a town and named it Marshall after Chief Justice Marshall of the U.S. Supreme Court whom both admired.

It was a time when numbers of well-to-do young easterners were heading west not to be settlers but to buy large parcels of land and make money. Politically savvy, they came knowing how to run a business and organize a meeting.

Two other bright young men, the Rev. John Pierce and a

lawyer, Isaac Cary, sat under an oak tree one day and worked out a school system for the future state. Cary became chairman of the state's first constitutional convention and was able to have his plans adopted as law. Then, not surprisingly, he became first superintendent of the new schools and a member of Congress.

By 1835 Marshall had a population of 300 and its first hotel, now the National House Inn. By 1840 this small Calhoun County town was so confident of being named capital of Michigan that a large plot marked "Capitol Square" was laid out and lots on the square were being sold at downtown Detroit prices. Senator James Wright Gorden, a former governor himself, built a handsome house to serve as a governor's mansion.

It wasn't just a fantasy. Detroit was the state capital when Michigan joined the Union in 1837 and the new state constitution decreed that the seat of Michigan government had to have a centralized location. Even citizens upstate thought Marshall (which sits nearly dead-center between east and west coasts) was a good choice.

It was not to be. Lansing, also central but farther north, won the capital blessing. Some say it was only by one vote, but that was enough. Deeply disappointed, Marshall citizens went on with their lives—which turned out to be pretty good ones in spite of deep economic woes.

Trouble brewing on a national scale had an early impact on Marshall when in 1846 Adam Crosswhite, an escaped slave living here with his family, was taken by force by his former owner. Incensed residents of Marshall rose up and arrested the slave hunters, ordering them back to Kentucky without Crosswhite. Then the former owner sued the Marshall folks and won. Those who took part in the rescue paid heavy fines while Crosswhite was whisked safely off to Canada.

The whole affair focused interest on the matter of fugitive slaves and some say this case stirred up greater fervor for the Civil War.

Marshall grew as an important shipping point and favorite dinner stop for the Michigan Central Railroad. Passengers were allowed twenty minutes to get off and find dinner in the mid-1800s; it took forty minutes to make the twelve-mile run to Albion. The oldest workers' union in the United States, the Brotherhood of the Footboard (now the Brotherhood of Locomotive Engineers) was conceived in the parlor of a Marshall home in 1863.

A decade later Michigan Central pulled a big switch by moving the rail yards to Jackson. This second blow to Marshall's general economy put progress into reverse gear.

Drugs brought on the next cash crisis—not the modern coke and crack scene, but the patent medicines on great grandma's bedroom table. Lydia Pinkham's Pink Pills for Pale People, among others, made fortunes for Marshall entrepreneurs.

Pills and potions of the late 1800s contained high levels of alcohol or opium and were sure to cure anything, including straight thinking. When the Pure Food and Drug Act (1906) was passed, however, home remedies with addictive—if not lethal—dosage recommendations had to be thrown down the privy pit. Lydia and her ilk went out of business.

Marshall swallowed its medicine once again.

Today's Marshall is both sedate and lively, oozing with civic pride. High-domed trees and wide streets set off the treasury of very special houses. While the fast-food and discount shopping are lumped near the west-side I-69 entrance, downtown Marshall has been adamant about not changing. Firmness has paid off as public buildings and residences—prime examples of their genre or one-of-a-kind gems—appear frequently in the national media.

The closeness of so many nineteenth-century homes and businesses (about 800 buildings) won the city distinction as the country's largest National Landmark Historic District, the highest rank given by the Interior's National Park Service.

It might have been different without Harold Brooks, mayor of Marshall in 1925. Brooks saw the value of preserving and restoring Marshall's architectural treasures in a time when everyone else could only think of modernizing. At one time Brooks owned twelve Marshall heritage buildings, having made a sizable fortune manufacturing rupture appliances. With zeal he hired landscape artists, gave out prizes for the best gardens, best lawns, best decorated houses, calling his efforts "city beautification" long before such phrases were household words.

To best enjoy the results of the Brooks influence, pick up a free walking tour map at the chamber of commerce office, 109 East Michigan Avenue. Downtown sidewalk trees are ringed with iron benches and have a pineapple, the symbol of hospitality, worked into the design. These are good places to sit and stare at the gentle Italianate architecture, the fresh paint on old surfaces. Chic boutiques, clothing stores, antique shops seem to dominate.

Include, if you can, an appointment to see the American Museum of Magic (616-781-7666) at 107 East Michigan, and meet owner-guide Robert Lund. Part wiz teacher, part kid, Lund does not tolerate tardiness or stupid questions asked twice. Yes, everything you see is real, from the Houdini gear to mementos of Fu-Manchu and Mandrake Comics.

In a fine little bookstore called the Kids' Place around the corner on Jefferson, over lunch in Ken's Café, in the Mole Hole gift shop, browse and ask directions.

Across from the Brooks Memorial Fountain (in the center of a traffic circle) stands a riveting piece of architecture called the Honolulu House, built in 1860 by Abner Pratt, a Marshall judge who became U.S. Consul to the Hawaiian Islands. Returning to Marshall because his wife was ill, Pratt kept wearing his white tropical suits and in 1860 built this house, designed to catch warm Pacific breezes . . . in case they blew toward Michigan.

Wide veranda, pagoda-like observation tower, lavish murals in jewel colors. Mr. Pratt filled his house with Polynesian souvenirs, exotic bric-a-brac, and a hopeless case of longing. Mrs. Pratt died soon after returning home, and Mr. Pratt followed her shortly. It was pneumonia, they say, induced by tropic delusions and not bundling up.

Today Honolulu House, listed in both the Historic American Building Survey and the National Register of Historic Places, continues life as a museum. Furnishings are not Pratt's, not even the folding bathtub made in Marshall. The house is located at 107 North

Honolulu House in Marshall

Kalamazoo Street and is open from mid-May through October, noon to 5:00 P.M.

Meander and gape at the beautiful Georgian colonials, Greek Revivals, Queen Anne specials; over one hundred houses are described in the walking tour brochure.

The *big* tour of the year was begun in 1954 by the ladies of Trinity Episcopal Church. What started as an annual kitchen tour (ironically to show off modernized kitchens in old houses) was so successful it was suggested that whole houses be opened up. By 1968 the popular affair was turned over to the Marshall Historical Society, and now 12,000 to 15,000 people come to view eight of Marshall's historic homes plus seven other vintage buildings.

Always the first weekend after Labor Day, festivities include a Civil War encampment, parade, brass band, church buffets, and much related hoopla. Tickets are available at the chamber of commerce; 800-877-5163. Designated as Michigan's "Christmas City," Marshall provides more home tours and a zillion lights down the streets and around the fountain during the holidays. Something Detroit-Chicago or Fort Wayne–Lansing commuters may want to detour for.

Another main Marshall event is dinner at Schuler's, a Michigan institution. Starting modestly as the dining room of a small hotel, jovial Win Schuler's enterprise, now run by his sons, has been a legend for decades. Super steaks, homemade bread, boar cheese, pie are among the specialties on the menu. Shuler's is found just south of Michigan Avenue on Eagle Street. It's a little pricey but worth it. For reservations call 616-781-0600.

Another spot to visit before leaving town is the National House Inn, 102 South Parkview (Fountain Circle). Built in 1835, only five years after Sidney Ketchum's arrival, this is the oldest operating inn in the state. Stagecoach stop, former Democratic headquarters, the National House is one of these "if walls could talk" places worth a book of its own. It's now a cheery bed and breakfast hostelry with updated comforts; call 616-781-7374. The proprietors are also on the chamber of commerce list of antique dealers.

Another bed and breakfast choice, McCarthy's Bear Creek

Inn, serves a large continental breakfast to their guests, who may be asked to sleep in the barn. That's good news. The barn on this farm home has been artfully remodeled into spacious bedrooms; located one mile west of Fountain Circle, 15120 C. Drive North. Telephone 616-781-8383. Full? There are plenty of motels on West Michigan Avenue.

Close enough to Marshall to be called a part of the scene is Cornwell's Turkeyville. Go north on I-69, past I-94 to the next exit to pens of gobblers and fine turkey dinners. Turkey Rueben, turkey salad, turkey chili, and no ham at the dinner theater. You'll also find a flea market, fairs, and anything the festive heart desires, but don't show up before 11:00 A.M. Telephone 616-781-4293.

Another interesting bit of Marshall trivia to take note of: buried in Marshall's Oakridge Cemetery is Samuel Hill, legendary aide to Douglass Houghton. Hill's swearing was so colorful that others took to merely using Sam's name instead of cussing things out. "What the Sam Hill!" was once mentioned by Robert Ripley in *Believe It Or Not*. Sam died in 1862.

Marshall doesn't miss being state capital at all.

Marshall Chamber of Commerce: 800-877-5163

16

Munising:
North Shore Landing

From the 1880s till the early 1930s, when cruise ships still puffed around the Great Lakes, Munising, on Lake Superior, was a favorite freshwater port of call, a tiny Odessa on an inland sea.

Describing the approach was enough to fill a dozen postcards. At a precautionary distance the ships passed massive cliffs (nearly 300 feet from the beach straight up to their crests), then steamed next to eerily eroded walls of multitoned rock rising from fifty to 200 feet above the water. After waving to a landmark lighthouse on Grand Island, passengers found themselves entering Munising's pretty little harbor, snug in the cupped hands of high green hills. A courthouse at the end of Elm Street where most business was done rose proudly above a bustling community devoted—as passengers would learn—to lumbering, fishing, mining, and tours through a wondrously scenic neighborhood.

The coming of a cruise ship was cause for another round of drinks. Custom dictated that the high-school band, all dressed up in their Sunday best, march down to the pier and play a welcome. Citizens stopped what they were doing to watch the SS *American*, for example, glide toward the dock. It could have been raining but skies were blue that day.

War and the Depression interrupted but Munising's future as a growing port and the seat of Alger County seemed destined.

The lovely old courthouse burned down, cruise ships were sold for scrap years ago. Today the high-school band wears uniforms when there's a football game against Marquette, but never to meet a boat. The population stands at a modest 3,500.

Lumbering and putting together wooden products (from log cabins to the best snowshoes ever made) is a big part of Munising's area income, but its booming claim to fame is as a gateway to the glorious Pictured Rocks National Lakeshore, the Alger Underwater Diving Preserve, and the newer undeveloped Grand Island Recreational Area.

Parks and recreation are a modern continuation of an ancient pattern. Long before the first European ventured into this sheltered cove, Munising was a Chippewa camp and religious site, where spirits of the dead soar in the form of eagles over the cliffs. Today the vibrations of faith in the face of creation are an individual matter, but reverence should come with the territory.

This is the legendary spot where Daughter-of-the-Moon, Nokomis, cared for little Hiawatha. Fringed with murmuring pines and hemlock, the sandstone hills spill over with waterfalls, evoking a dream of Minnie Ha Ha, the maiden whose name meant "sparkling waters" and the love of Hiawatha's manhood. Wagner, Horsehoe, and Munising Falls are only a few blocks from midtown.

On the east side of town near the water's edge, State 28 takes a sharp turn. Facing the road (County 58) entering this curve from the east are the Hiawatha National Forest–Pictured Rocks National Lakeshore Visitors Center (PRNL), a state-police station, and the Munising Visitors Center. Beyond them are the stacks of a Kimberly Clark paper mill and the path upward to the gates of the National Lakeshore.

The PRNL Center explains the area's logging history and rock strata, and sells books and pamphlet guides to flora and fauna, lighthouses or waterfalls, or Great Lakes lore. Temporarily housed in a large mobil unit, Munising's welcome center will shower you with lists, folders, giveaway papers, guides. Even if you announce plans to explore the woods via dogsled in August, they'll just hand you a route map.

The hills lend Munising enchantment; however, it must be said in candor and honesty, the town will not move the architecturally sensitive to tears. Its plain, hardworking heritage had little time for fancies; an immigrant population put up practical homes and stores, largely without much gingerbread or frills. (I'm speaking of Munising's general ambience, not of modern pleasures such as the indoor pool and in-room Jacuzzi at the Comfort Inn.)

This is the north country, where facing into tough times has been as regular a feature as the coming of winter. That the citizens are so universally friendly and cheerful tells you what matters and what doesn't matter to them. It's hard not to feel at home.

As of this writing the big white Victorian house that served as a historical museum is being replaced by larger quarters in the rehabilitated old Washington School. Nineteenth-century documents, photos, bric-a-brac, bustles, and ore picks, plus an 1840 fur trader's cabin from Grand Island, now look toward the spot where the museum originally sat. True research should include listening to some of the tapes with voices of Munising old-timers telling about the way it was.

The city that started with an iron smelter and pot has parts of its past living a new life deep in icy Lake Superior. The Alger Underwater Preserve is a choice Great Lakes site for exploring old shipwrecks or subsurface caves. Reaching from Au Train Point on the west to Au Sable Point on the east a roll call of lost vessels includes the *Superior*, a side-wheel steamer wrecked in 1856, with fragments spread over a large area; the *Kiowa*, a steel steamer whose hull lies in three pieces; and the *Smith Moore*, a dramatic 230-foot hulk of a steam barge, the most intact wreck of all. There are half a dozen others. Call the Grand Island Charters for diving information: 906-387-4477. Just remember that it's *very* illegal to take home shipwreck souvenirs.

A top Michigan excursion is the Pictured Rocks Boat Tour, leaving from a midtown Munising dock. Only over a boat rail can you see these surprisingly colorful rock walls, carved by ice and water into caves and arches, forts and profiles (use your imagination), some of them dripping with green-blue oxides and mineral tints. I would advise taking the two-and-a-half-hour thirty-seven-mile round-trip late in the day during July to catch the sun on the rainbow surfaces, but anytime is better than missing this dramatic slice of Michigan geology.

Tours are run from the Friday before Memorial Day to the first weekend in October, with only two cruises in June and September; call 906-387-2379.

Check in to the Best Western Four Seasons (906-387-4864) on State 28 East, or Scotty's Motel (906-387-2449) on Cedar Street, among nine or ten others, and plan a one-day jaunt to Grand Marais, Singleton, and back. It may say something about local conditions in winter when four motels here like to advertise their heated car repair facilities.

Below the lake, on top of the lake, above the lake; there is another world above those cliffs and the mammoth dunes beyond their eastern limits. The Pictured Rocks National Lakeshore has to be seen, hiked along, wondered over. Three miles at its widest point and over forty miles long, the park's ample spaces hug the top of the cliffs, a low forested point, and miles of dunes cresting nearly 300 feet above the water.

Detours from County 58 will take you over miles of gravel road that only *seem* endless until you are drenched in the dappled beauty of a birch forest or spot a bear rambling off into the distance. In due time you reach breathtaking views of Lake Superior at Miners Castle or the log slide overlook. I can't over-recommend a pause at Sable Falls and a walk up to the top of the Grand Sable Dunes, my favorite spot in the whole world. Or go to Woodland Park in Grand Marais and hike west along the beach. Most of these views have handicapped access; the visitors center has details. (The east end visitors center closes at the end of summer.)

Delightful little Grand Marais has gone from boomtown of 2,500 souls and thirty saloons in 1890 to the edge of oblivion, and ironically has had to fight off spoilers who think it would make a great resort spot. Condos and a golf course would be like putting

Hiking at Pictured Rocks

go-carts in a museum. This is a village hanging on to its timeless-ness; it's a gem at the end of the road. About as jumping as they want to get is the Bluegrass Festival in August.

Close to the water a great little ice-cream parlor (there's only one so details aren't necessary) scoops up the ice cream of your dreams. Nearby, Lefebvre's Fish Market smokes its fish and turkey specialties over hardwood and sells the cheese and dark bread needed for a gourmet lunch; 906-494-2563. Vows to come back soon are made over and over at Lefebvre's. There are rooms for about 200 overnighters in midsummer. Usually they are filled, but call Munising for information.

Take State 77 south to Seney (on the outskirts of a large wildlife refuge) then west on a drawing board-straight twenty-five-mile piece of road known to natives as the Seney-Singleton Stretch. If Iverson's snowshoe manufacturing place is open as you drive through Singleton, stop in for a friendly tour of a rare operation. The factory can be found on Maple Street; 906-452-6370.

Back in Munising, with about one hundred additional miles on your car, home cooking is guaranteed at Ziegert's, Leach's, or the Dogpatch. Reservations are never needed.

The latest Munising area attraction is still wilderness. Grand Island, just offshore, a large club-shaped piece of real estate with a hammerhead peninsula on the east side, is now public land with an uncertain future. Apparently, there will be no development until the environmentalists and others make their case.

Barely west of Munising on County 28 lies Christmas, a real place, that serves to remind summer travelers that this is a winter wonderland too, with many miles of groomed cross-country ski and snowmobile trails.

Popular annual events include snowshoe races, a winter carnival, and an interesting-sounding Moose Flea Market in July. Think I'll try that sometime.

Alger County–Munising Chamber of Commerce: 906-387-2138
Pictured Rocks National Lakeshore: 906-387-3700

17

Rogers City: Courage in a Quiet Place

Magnificent sweeping mirrors to the sky, moody sweetwater wonders, the Great Lakes have come to be deeply respected by experienced sailors. Their waves can break a ship, especially during the gales of November, a season of swift, fierce, freezing storms. Any vessel with a weakness becomes a target for disaster, evidenced by hundreds of wrecks (including the *Edmund Fitzgerald*) scattered across the lakes' dark floors.

Few towns know more about the awesome strength of the lakes than Rogers City, a joyful, outgoing community on northern Lake Huron; and a place with tragic memories.

It was November, 1958, when a limestone ore ship, the *Carl D. Bradley*, was returning after delivering its last load of the season. Limestone is a big Rogers City product; the *Bradley* had received praise for being one of the safest ships on the inland seas, although this was disputed by later evidence.

The Rogers City captain and crew never made it home. A sudden gale stirred upper Lake Michigan into a hellish icy caldron. The *Bradley* broke up and sank; only two survived.

With a population of less than 4,000, Rogers City became the port on the Great Lakes with the greatest percentage per capita of fatherless children.

That was a generation ago, mentioned in private moments or on memorial days. Yet visitors should be aware.

The largest community in Presque Isle County is another water-country town. Sitting along the east coast where it curves toward the Straits of Mackinac, Rogers City lies between miles of forest, a surprising amount of farmland, not too many people, and a wide, blue horizon.

Lake Huron is second largest of the Great Lakes supporting small cities and towns on its shore but no sprawling metro areas like Chicago, Milwaukee, or even Muskegon. Alpena, thirty-eight miles south with 12,000 people, is as urban as it gets. (Bay City's center faces the Saginaw River not the lake, but true, it *is* the largest Huron port.)

"Nautical City," the nickname Rogers City citizens have chosen, has come a long way since 1839, when a surveying party sent out by the state declared the region worthless. Rivers were shallow and crooked, there didn't seem to be any minerals of value, and the soil (such as wasn't covered by trees) appraised as poor for farming.

Yet in the 1860s an intrepid family named Crawford settled into the quiet cove where Rogers City is now located. They intended to open a stone quarry, but instead made a living selling wood fuel to steamboats. It took folks with money to invest to come build a sawmill and store, establishing a company town, the Molitor-Rogers Company. It was an isolated life without roads to the rest of the state. Even the stolid Polish and German families who came up on ships to live independently on farms, fishing boats, or as lumberjacks had to go to the company for all supplies. Yet, like a seedling in a rock crevice, Rogers City grew.

It took the vast deposits of limestone (a material vital to the making of steel) to push further settlement. The Michigan Limestone and Chemical Company bought Crawford's old quarry, along with 8,000 additional acres; the Bradley Transportation Company took the stone on long freighters to Gary, Indiana, River Rouge, Toledo, Cleveland, and the smelters of the east.

A platform for visitors overlooks the world's largest limestone quarry (5,000 acres) in action—not swift action to be sure, but a "dance" of bulldozers, placement of dynamite, and everyone clearing out. The blast goes off. Huge shovels remove the rock, now 250 feet below the one-time surface.

From the "harbor view" you can watch chunks being sorted by size and see freighters loaded. (The last load on the *Carl Bradley* filled up three complete freight trains.) Call 517-734-2117 to learn shipping schedules.

Smaller craft come and go from the Rogers City Waterways Commission Marina like puppies to a feed bowl. This is a "Harbor of Refuge" town, an official designation when the state decided no sailor should have to cope with more than thirty miles of coast between shelters.

The marina merges with a city park where a beach, tennis courts, playground, and picnic tables make a great place for watching boats or people. A band shell hosts free concerts once in a while and at all special events, such as the Fourth of July. They save fireworks for the Nautical City Festival during the first week of August.

Both the Nautical Fest and the Salmon Tournament draw big crowds. For the tourney, however, the crowd hunches over with a certain fanaticism. Plans are laid; all charter boats rented. "Best spot" information is passed in secret code—it seems. Through September, the tasty, challenging chinook salmon takes over all waking, thinking hours of a fisherman's brain.

Several years ago the Department of Natural Resources planted salmon in enormous numbers from their hatchery at Swan Creek. The payoff earned Rogers City the "Salmon Capital" nickname that's not too far off the mark.

Coho, pink salmon, brown trout are plentiful in the spring; talk fish till you grow fins. This is the place. However, anyone who didn't come by boat or has no gear can buy fresh, smoked, or filleted, from a third-generation fish dealer. Gauthier & Spaulding Fisheries has retail space on US 23, recently enlarged; 517-734-3474. Near the older docks are the decaying fishing boat hulks, remnants of big commercial years.

More menu makings are available at Plath's Meat Market, famed for pork loin straight from the smokehouse out back and located at 116 South Third, another grandfather-established trade; 517-734-2232.

Downtown Rogers City is quiet and pleasant, no challenge to anyone in decent walking shoes. A town centerpiece, the Avenue of Flags, was dedicated in 1977. At first, thirty (or so) shipping-company flags fluttered the logos of merchant "lakers," but today a number of national banners have replaced the commercial ones.

Trivia devotees may note that Rogers City heard the first ship-to-shore broadcasts heard on the lakes back in 1922 when few ships were equipped with radios. Station WLC has been heard ever since.

The Presque Isle Historical Society Museum turns out to be a handsome bungalow house on Second Street, filled with memorabilia from Roger City's incredibly hardworking beginnings: flapper-day hats, period furnishings, and in the basement a prize—a true Indian birch bark canoe gliding silently on its own stream of time. Telephone 517-734-4121.

Rogers City has one movie house and one county courthouse, both serving the whole county. It wasn't always this way. When the county was organized and Rogers City designated as Presque Isle county seat (500 people lived here then) it was felt that the folks at the far western side of the county weren't being properly served, so a second court was set up in Onaway, complete with courthouse.

It sounded good, but the litigants, witnesses, and lawyers too often would show up in good faith at the wrong place. Onaway was closed.

The name "Presque Isle" means "almost an island," and originally referred to the rocky knob just north of Alpena. Two historic lighthouses stand guard there. The oldest, a short but sturdy sentry, was built in 1840 and abandoned thirty years later when a new lighthouse went up a mile to the north. Visitors can climb the stone steps of the old lighthouse for a scenic view, and

The oldest lighthouse on nearby Presque Isle

go through the keeper's house, furnished with unusually fine relics. For a time Jefferson Davis was believed to have been the architect of the old light, but that rather romantic notion has been disproven.

Restoration is currently going on at the "new" Presque Isle light so it may be closed. Nothing stops you from walking around the grounds to take pictures.

In the back county, driving though 74,000 acres of state forest can seem endless, but with a state map you might want to seek out Ocqueoc Falls, the largest in the lower peninsula. Not spectacular, but a very pretty run of white water in a beautiful area. Signs of cross-country ski trails and snowmobile routes give their own come-back suggestions.

Return in early September when tiny Posen—300 souls, more or probably less—puts on a potato festival out of all proportion to the village size. Fifteen miles south of Rogers City, Posen's Polish farmers have been polka-ing through a fete that now draws 25,000 or so spectators and features a milelong parade plus a potato pancake smorgasbord (a Swedish word. So what?). Visitors can buy hundred-pound sacks of spuds for $8.00. The limestone soil is said to give them extra flavor.

Back at Rogers City, golf addicts find relief at the Rogers City Country Club, 425 Golf Course Road. There are nine holes today; they hope to have another nine someday, but not quite yet. Call 517-734-4909.

Food, the real thing, not just what the café says it is, but true home cooking, is available at a terrific family dining room called Kortman's Restaurant; 517-734-3512. Chi-Chi's Restaurant also caters to the home and family crowd; 517-734-4454. For special times, Jason's is dressier, more elegant; 517-734-4531. There are several motels and area resorts but a distinct shortage of bed and breakfasts in the area.

The route from Rogers City northward has the grace of emptiness, quiet scenery, nearly deserted beaches. Seagull Point Nature Area offers a nature trail and beach. Hoeft State Park has the widest beach with the smallest crowds anywhere. Ten people would be a crowd on the days I've been there, but I'm sure this beauty spot must have busy times.

Forty Mile Point does it again. The tranquil bluff forty miles from Mackinaw City has been a landmark for more than 200 years. A two-and-a-half-story lighthouse, not open to visitors, stands over picnic facilities and plenty of breathing room. It is a place to watch the long ships passing, this time with more respect. Knowing something of Rogers City does that to you.

Rogers City Chamber of Commerce: 517-734-2535

Index

Index

Index

Index

Other titles in the Country Towns series:

County Towns of Arkansas
Country Towns of Georgia
Country Towns of Michigan
Country Towns of New York
Country Towns of Northern California
Country Towns of Pennsylvania

Spring 1995
Country Towns of Connecticut and Rhode Island
Country Towns of Florida
Country Towns of Louisiana
Country Towns of Maine
Country Towns of Southern California
Country Towns of Texas

All books are $9.95 at bookstores.
Or order directly from the publisher (add $3.00 shipping and
handling for direct orders):

Country Roads Press
P.O. Box 286
Castine, Maine 04421
Toll-free phone number: **800-729-9179**